10 Items or Less

10

Items or Less

Life in the Fast Lane

An eye opening look into the unusual
behavior of everyday grocery shoppers

by Scott Omel

INTRODUCTION

"Hello, how are you today?" This is the greeting that so many have heard when shopping at the supermarket. Millions of times I have asked this question, and I have meant it every time. Unfortunately, we only have a moment to spend together before we must move on with our busy lives.

So begins each of my many tales, as I have observed the brief views into the lives and personalities of the people who have graced us with their patronage.

In my book "10 Items or Less, Life in the Fast Lane", I offer a glimpse into the outrageous live productions of the micro reality shows that people offer, as they shop throughout the store and make their way through the checkout.

As you'll see from peering through my eyes upon these events, that people feel comfortable at the supermarket and act as they normally do and not in a publicly refined way. This has led to the buildup of numerous eye-opening experiences that finally boiled within me to the point that I had to open up and share them with you.

So, here in my book, I give the rare opportunity to peek into many brief accounts and my commentary of the intriguing behavior of the people that surround us all, as they try to squeeze their way through life in the fast lane. You may even see a glimpse of yourself in here too!

Thank you for shopping, and please come again....

10 ITEMS OR LESS

LIFE IN THE FAST LANE

Chasing you into the depths, the piercing grip of the hour hand grasps you away from the reaches of your mind, while you beg the minute hand for mercy. You subtly attempt to compose yourself from your ethereal travels, before the sunrise unfolds upon another day. As you primp in your own uncongenial fashion, who do you purport to be?

Why, unbeknownst to thyself, you are star of the show! As we whisk you up upon center stage to present your monologue we are the cast and crew, and we have been waiting for your arrival. We were up before the dawn, and will burn the oil until twilight in preparation for your scene. You are a star of life itself, which is the most captivating play of them all. The lights are shining upon you despite being completely unaware of your exhibition. As you meander your way up to the counter, you ask, "Mirror, mirror on the wall, do I have ten items or less?" Little did you know, it is I, behind the mirror, hung in a way to reflect who you really are. So in reply I say, "Yes, you are the fairest of them all."

I've come to realize after 25 years at the grocery store,

that it is a place unlike any other in its position to view humanity as it really is. It would seem to be out of bounds, as it were, because it is not part of the outside world, but an extension of the home. People do not act as they would in public, they act as though they are in familiar surroundings. I can best illustrate my observation by use of this particular experience:

One day, while I was working in the checkstand, a little old lady comes through my line buying various items, and she was dressed in her morning garb. I looked over the counter and noticed that she had on her fuzzy slippers, her terrycloth robe, some kind of goop on her face, and her hair in curlers. So, being sarcastically curious, I inquired about her choice of dress. She replied to me, "This is so I will look good, when I go out." "I see", I replied. I did not have the heart to tell her, that she actually was "out". But it was then, that I realized, that she did not believe that she was out, and it began to explain all the other unusual activities that people do. Most feel right at home, to do as they please, while at the grocery store.

Now, each time I take my place at work, I feel a sense of pride, knowing that it takes a certain kind of person to work at the market. For a moment, you become part of their home, like a guest. As you take your place, you are the "mirror, mirror on the wall". You are there, but you are not. You are their reflection, but you are also a personality hidden behind the mirror, peering into their lives. What a great position to view the live reality shows.

"It is a love 'em or hate 'em kind of job". That is what I tell all the new hires as they come and try their luck at pleasing the masses. Working with the public is interesting of course, but it seems to be further pronounced at the supermarket. I continue to tell them that people will either get on your nerves until you quit, or you will find them oddly entertaining and get a weird pleasure out of dealing with them day to day. Our regular customers are wonderful, but it is the odd ones that make for good entertainment.

No matter what, you have to be pleasant at all times despite any personal problems or feelings you may be experiencing. You must be able to greet each and every person individually and treat them as if they were special for that moment. Don't forget, they have let you into their home, sort of speak, and if you don't give them personal attention, oh my, that's a mistake! Sometimes you are trying so hard to just get people through the checkstand, that you start to run them all together, but then you get that look. It is the look that says, aren't you going to say hello to me? Am I not standing right here in front of you? Right then, you are caught in your fauxpas, and quickly gather yourself together and say, "So, how are you today?"

Although it seems longer when you are waiting in line, most orders take less than a minute to complete. Even so, if you do not say a greeting, it is like seeing family and not saying hello. A major mistake for sure, because all it takes is one person to complain about you or send a letter to the office, and you will be reprimanded, transferred, suspended or even fired, depending on the extent of your error. So, "Who is the fairest of them all"? You are, the one who is standing right in front of me.

Somehow, I knew that in one way or another, everyone has had some sort of odd experience in the express lane, but I didn't realize that it was such a hot topic, until I was reading "Dear Abby" recently. Somebody voiced comment about certain troublesome behavior they witnessed in the speed lane, and it prompted a flood of letters in reply.

Despite the short amount of time, it is interesting to see the relationships that develop with people you only see for a minute or two, once a week or so. Some clerks are amazing. I remember one gal I worked with, who knew me since I was five years old shopping with my mother. She could remember customer's names, their children's names, and could pick up and continue in a conversation with a customer days later, like opening to a bookmark in a novel. There would be people in her line, and I would say to them, "I can help you over here in another lane." They would reply, "No, thank you, I'm here to see Jackie." It's impressive to see somebody, who is so proficient with people.

As I've collected these thoughts and experiences, I always said, I would one day write a book about all the people and things I've seen while working at the store, although I never thought that I would actually do it. But the other day after my latest encounter, I came to the conclusion that I could not hold back from telling everyone, about the stories and scenes that have played out right in front of me. I have seen it all, ... and then I go back to work, and I am shocked once again! So, as I tell you about all of these things, you may find them as entertaining as I have, and you may even see yourself in here too.

I don't know where to start, really, so I guess I will begin with the concept itself. In an effort to make improvements, we always lose a little along the way. Like anything else, times change, and so do people. Therefore, the way people do things changes over the years too, with so much comedy to be found along the way.

When I first came on board and began working at the store, the express lane was still fairly a new thing, and most people abided by the concept. It originally would read, "10 items or less, cash only". However, those with that rebellious spirit felt the urge to flex their American freedom and like a fast draw, would reach for their leather and ask, "Will you take a check?" "Sure, we take all nationalities." I reply. So, here it began. The beginning of the downfall of what was supposed to be an advancement in society to save us all sorts of valuable time. It is a reflection of the world itself, so advanced, and yet at a loss to know where all of our time went.

I remember when I first saw the end result of a certain technological advancement. Do you recall, when the cell phone used to be this large box you had to carry with you, and the handset still had the cord attached? Well, way back then, I saw a guy on the baking aisle looking up and down the shelf, saying to his wife on the other line, "I don't see the cake mix you want." It was then that I knew, that the sole purpose of the cell phone was to make sure that a husband would finally bring home the correct items from the store that his wife wanted!

It still happens though. You have never seen a more downtroddened look on someone's face, than the husband, who has been sent back to the store by his wife, because he brought home the wrong thing. I feel especially sympathetic for the men, who have been sent in for tampons, but are not quite certain exactly which ones his wife uses. He'll be back, I'm sure.

Well, it is time to clock in and join the battle. As we wait for the last tick, we try to hide ourselves from the leers of all the people waiting in line, wondering when we are going to start work and get them out of here. Our nerves are preparing for flight, as the air of jittery impatience among the customers seems like they all are coming down off two cups of Starbucks. The caffeinated pace burns out some employees quickly, but nervous cats, like myself, thrive in such an atmosphere. My secret? I keep little chocolates in my apron. It also doesn't hurt to slip my fellow employees one or two, when their tanks are running low. So, as I get started and open another register, the customers wash in upon my checkstand like refugees coming off the boat. I'm like Coast Guard rescue! Every time I open up, I get a heroic welcome.

As you quickly learn in a job serving the public, there are rules of etiquette that you should apply. One of the first things I tell the new ones as a rule of thumb. Don't ever say "ma'am" or "sir", because you might be wrong. I've seen it happen many a time. One of the baggers looks over to the customer unloading their cart and says, "Hello sir, would you like paper or plastic?" Then you see the head turn with a snarled look, and granted, she does look like Oscar the grouch, but oops, the he is actually a she! That always gets an interesting response, from everyone involved. The customer gives the look like, "Are you talking to me?" The bagger shrugs his shoulders mumbling, how was I supposed to know? ....And me, I always get a good chuckle as the innocent spectator. Well, I guess it is like my daddy used to say,

"Make sure you check under the hood!"

It is so hard to tell these days. There are a couple regulars in my store, who are either "pre-op" or who simply cross dress and take hormones. They are cordial, but I always like to see their response, when a new employee throws them a ma'am or sir. Sometimes, I peek at the name they have chosen. It is always a neutral one like Blair, Chris, or simply their initials. I always check the "Adam's apple". That's the giveaway.

Years ago, we had a few transvestite men, who would come shopping early in the morning dressed in their raunchy street wear after finishing their "evening work", and needing a shave and a new set of pantyhose. Somehow, I could never find the right words to begin any conversation. "How was work?" was definitely out and I didn't want to start anything, because some are built like NFL football players! Sometimes, it is best to just smile and keep to yourself.

Beginning conversation and chit chat can sometimes be a little tricky, but there are some basic guidelines to remember. There is one special rule that applies, but especially to men. Woman can get away with this inquiry and come away unscathed, but if a guy like myself leans over the counter and asks a woman, "How far along are you?" Boy, you are walking on thin ice! Now granted, if they are in their eighth or ninth month, and they appear to have a watermelon under their shirt and have the push button belly button, then you are pretty much safe. But, I remember one lady that came through. I saw her belly and had contemplated asking about her new arrival, but chose the course of wisdom and stuck to a neutral subject. On the other hand, one of the female employees who was bagging for me, leaned over and asked when she was due? The customer quickly became a bit huffy and responded, "I am not pregnant!" I just rolled my eyes up and gave the bagger the look of my restrained laughter! That's definitely a no, no.

It is just these types of rules that create the atmosphere that makes it possible for me to share these expressions with you. If everybody followed the rules and did just the right thing, then my day would not be quite as lively. It is the breaking of rules and still trying to fit in, is the challenge that so many take on. Everybody loves to make new rules for others, but for themselves, …..well, we could bend that one a little, just for you.

When I was in school, one of the new trends they were initiating upon youngsters was the "self esteem" programs. We were all taught that we are special, and that nobody should do or say anything that should make us feel less about ourselves. Meanwhile, years down the road, everyone struts about as "king of the castle" or "queen of the kingdom". Now, everyone is a bit inflated with self esteem, the end result, reality T.V. So, as some of the well trained count their items to see if they qualify for the special rate of "10 items or less", along comes the spoiler, who ruins it for everybody.

"I thought I had less than ten.", "I'm in a big hurry.", "I didn't want to wait in the other line.", "Oh, I shop here all the time, you know me.", "I'm sorry, I didn't see the sign.", the latter being the most common response. I give them a nod that there might be some truth to their story, but the evidence remains, in that, I already saw them look up at the sign before they entered the line. Wanting to corner them in their lie, I instead bite my tongue and tickle their ears saying, Yes.....you are the fairest of them all.

These days, the express lane has really become a thing of the past, because more than half of the people that come through the line should not actually be there. The past couple decades have people asserting their individuality and thrusting it upon others, but there is a new contender that has washed in and is drowning all the rest, ...The oblivious ones! Yes the state of complete unawareness of your surroundings is the wave of the future. Now, people simply flow wherever their feet take them no matter where they go. These ones enter right into the express lane unknowingly, because their minds are completely engaged elsewhere, and that wonderful place of oblivion is generally entered through the cell phone!

Some people have a valid excuse, such as restless children or a real handicap, but most offenders simply have mindless disregard. So many people these days are shopping at the store, but their minds are somewhere else. The distance has been increased dramatically by use of the cell phone. They are so far away, that they don't even realize how rude they are being to everyone. They enter the express lane, unload their items with their only good hand one at a time, fumble through their wallets and purses with a krink in their neck holding their phone, pay for their items after finally comprehending my hand signals, then are shuffled along to make room for everybody else, who have been leering at them trying to send ESP, telling them to get off the phone!!

They never knew that they were completely annoying to everyone, just total oblivion! It is hard to know exactly what to do in this situation. I don't want to be rude and interrupt their conversation. It might be important. But usually after a bit of eavesdropping, it isn't. Sometimes I'll get two blinks which means hello. Some revert to their childlike shopping ways. They come through, holding their cash or cards in the air, and they simply let me take their money or plastic and complete their order, not knowing what they were charged for or how much. They show the complete trustingness of a child hoping that us adults will take care of everything. So, what does it all mean? Times have changed. Get out of the way all of you scofflaws, dumbnation is coming through!

Here's a recent example. A guy just came through my line holding his phone to his ear with his shoulder. He doesn't acknowledge my existence or the position in line he has acquired. After ringing up his stuff, I give him hand signals in an attempt to draw money out of him, before I shuffle him along. He pulls a wad of cash out of one pocket and fiddles through it. Then he pulls out another wad out of his other pocket and does the same. All the while, he is on the phone, apparently with some sort of creditor regarding his accounts. He is actually complaining to them about how they leave him on hold and transfer him around. Then, to capture the moment entirely, he has the nerve to say to the person on the other end of the phone, "....You know, time is money, and you keep wasting my time!" I wish I could have taken the surveillance video and played it back to him as myself and all the other customers in line behind him show our complete agreement of his own words, as we stand there waiting for him to get off the phone and pay up. As we all stare at him, he still hasn't given me any money. While still on the phone, he observes his wads of bills and decides that he wants to give me the exact dollar amount. So, he pulls out his wallet and gives me the, "one potato, two potato" thing, until he finally paid up and left without any acknowledgement. Unbelievable, we all thought and commented, as I continued with the next orders.

Another side effect of cell phone technology took affect a few years ago. In years past, when we would see somebody come into the store and start mumbling things to themselves and talking out loud to nobody as they wandered aimlessly through the store, we would say, oh no, one of the local transients has come in. They are out of liquor and are conversing with their hallucinated friend.

Then one day, I look over to see a girl carrying a hand basket walking around the store aimlessly and talking to herself out loud, gesturing, and so forth. I thought to myself, "She is too well dressed and decent looking to be a transient", and then she turned to the side to reveal the cause of her aimlessness,......Bluetooth! Nowadays, alongside all the transients are those, who are inebriated wirelessly, trying to prove that you can focus your mind on two things at once, but failing miserably. Well, they may be hands free, but they are definitely not mind free. They tend to be even worse than the cell phone oblivion crowd. They will be looking right at me and talking, but don't even know I exist. Some will try to converse with me and someone else on the phone at the same time. Sorry, no two timers!

So, back to the express lane we go, where it was determined awhile back, that most people do not have 10 items or less, nor do they have cash. Being that we are in an industry, that gives the customers what they want, or you could just call it inflation, the express lane fattened itself to 15 items or less, and you may pay with whatever you've got. Great, don't you think? Well, its effect went over in like manner as government projects, in that it just further complicated an already problematic situation. It is just like my friends, who are always late. Even if you told them to meet at 8 o'clock instead of 7:00, they would still be late. Giving them the extra leeway didn't correct their problem, it just extended it. So, extra room was given to those, who may have had a difficulty adhering to 10 items or less, not realizing that if they can't count to 10, they definitely can't count to 15! Now, it's just a crap shoot. People stop counting after they run out of fingers, and so they just dump their stuff on the counter and say, " I think it's less than 15". What can we do? Just as I have done in the past, I just put my head down and keep 'em moving,.......''Rawhide.''

It is either feast or famine up front in the checkstand, people are like a school of fish. When one turns, they all turn. One minute it is quiet and there are few people in line. Next, everybody charges to the front, and they all want out this minute! So, I'll give you an insider tip. There is always a surge of people leaving the store at the top of the hour. I'm not sure why, but that's how it is.

O.k., I've got a good rhythm going, and now everybody

is moving. Then, there is always one, full of gumption, that has just a couple items, is friendly and chatty, but then, as if by surprise, pulls out a bag full of goods, plops them on the counter and says, "I would like to return these".

Oh nooooo!!!! As my eyebrows are thrust upwards and my eyes peer to the persons behind her in line, I see the great sigh amongst them all, knowing that the "express" has just been wiped off of the "express lane" and I infer with a glance, "I didn't know…..it wasn't my fault!" Somehow, people get the impression that the inversion of the signage also applies, in that you can return 15 items or less too. People know better, or else they wouldn't surprise you with it. But like any business, the grocery store loves to sell you things, but they hate taking things back, so they have mounds of paperwork in triplicate you have to fill out in order to return anything. The conveyer belt stops and out comes the paperwork. "Manager key service!"

Even with all that, I try my best to keep things going anyway. One day, a guy that was a bit peeved, when I proceeded to ring up a customer with excessive items, spoke up and said what most people feel. He asked, "Why doesn't anybody enforce the rules around here? Anyone who has more than 10 items in this line should be thrown out!" As I hurriedly continued with his order, I tried to explain that this wasn't an actual "law" that we enforce, but that it's more of a suggestion that we recommend in order to expedite the purchase process. I was fairly impressed with my reply, although it really didn't make him feel any better. Everyone would have liked it better if I had just thrown her out.

Oh my, you should have seen the crew that just came through. There were five adults with a half a cart of groceries. They saw that my line was short, so they crowded in and engaged in that ghetto style, toss out lines, kind of conversation that somehow includes me. One says, "Hey, 'dis is 'da express lane." Another says, "We're close to the limit." A third directs a line toward me saying, "You'll take us, won't ya'?", with that "woe is me" tone. Realizing that it would take more time to try to get them out of my line then to just take them, I motioned them forward. That was a mistake, because they were going to "get me sucka'!" So, away I go, and the tally is rolling. Mama tells me to watch the total, because she doesn't want to go over $75. No problem, so I stop at $74. She tells me to keep going. I figure that she is going to do like others, and dig into her private reserve she has stashed in her brassiere. O.k., your total is $101. Then back we go throwing the lines around. "Pappy said to only spend $80." "You'd betta' do what pappy says." "No, it's o.k. He won't mind." "If pappy says $80, it betta' be $80. Don't you go over" "You'd betta' call pappy." Oh man, this is ridiculous. So, the bunch of them keep mulling over what to do, and what pappy is going to say if they go over, and these were middle aged adults!

So, the one that was calling pappy on her cell phone, to see if they could spend an extra $20, decided that it would be better not to even ask, and hung up. By this time, I had turned off the light to my checkstand and basically closed it up. A couple unlucky ones, who were next in line, figured out this was going to be awhile, so they picked up there stuff and went to a different register. Meanwhile, we move on to the next act of our play. They start pulling out items one at a time for me to deduct from the total. I had to get the manager to come and help me void these items. They don't trust us to void our own items anymore. Of course, I have to write down each item that I am voiding, to explain myself to the boss at a future time. Finally, we have the total down to $73. Why we just didn't stop here in the first place, I really don't know. O.k., just when I think we are finally getting somewhere, she pulls out her EBT food stamp card. "That worked o.k., so now your total is $7.55". "7.55? Why do we owe you $7.55?" "Well, you can't buy hot fried chicken with your food stamp card." They start tossing lines again. "How come we can't buy chicken?" "Anybody got $7?" "Forget it, just take off the chicken." They give me the box of chicken, that isn't hot anymore, because they have been dragging it around the store. It just ends up in the garbage, because we can't re-sell it. Then, once again, I have to call a manager to deduct more off of their bill. It was a sorry display. As I was watching them, and kicking myself in the butt for my own stupidity for letting them come through my line, I couldn't believe that five grown adults couldn't, or wouldn't somehow come up with $7. I would have even thrown in the .55 cents just to get 'em outa' here! Holy cow. It was disgraceful.

Just recently, after another gentleman came through following a full cart family, he commented that, "If nobody follows the sign, then you should just take it down!" So, I replied that I am going to add a clause to the signage that says, "Optional". At least I got a laugh out of him before he left.

You can't win, by the way. There is no right thing to do. One of the girls I worked with actually did kick someone out of the express lane and make her take her goods off of the register and move to a regular checkstand, and the customer just about blew her top! She called for a manager and explained how humiliated she felt. Of course, a checkstand was then opened just for her, and the employee was reprimanded for not providing good customer service. You can't tell a customer that they are wrong anymore, or else they will have a conniption, then utter the newest of my favorite lines….."Where is the manager?"

There was one manager that stood out from all the rest. He was a bit high strung and "in your face" kind of thing, but he was fair. He was all over you if you did something wrong, but he would commend you for doing something right. He was unorthodox, but he ran a good tight store, and he never asked anyone to work harder than he did. He was the best manager I had ever worked for. Then one day, he stood up to do the greatest act of management I have ever seen.

We had a regular customer, who was a large, loud, rough, and round lady, who made all employees cringe when she came pounding up to the checkstand. Some of the clerks would actually call management to ring up her groceries instead, while they stepped aside, due to her sour demeanor. They couldn't take the abuse she would dish out. She would yell at us saying, "Don't start ringing up my groceries until I get over there and watch you, because you are going to overcharge me for everything!!" She would then question us on every item that we keyed in, making us tell her how much, or how much per pound, just to make sure. Then when we bagged her order, she would again bite our ear, "Don't put the glass jar of apple juice on the bottom, it might get broken!! Put the bread on the bottom and put the glass jar on top of the bread (squishing the bread) so that it doesn't break!!" You get the idea. We became used to her, as much as we could.

So, one day, it was as busy as can be, and she came through the line in her usual tyrannical manner and unloaded a verbal barrage that brought the girl in the checkstand to tears. So, when this particular manager came up to attend to the matter, he saw whom it was, and assessed what had happened.

He then proceeded to point his finger at that customer and let her have it in fine managerial style. Right in front of all the customers, he chastised her and explained, "If you have a problem with anyone or anything in my store, you come to me! That is why I am the manager!! Now get out of my store, and don't come back until you have learned some manners!" He threw her out of the store! He turned to the clerk that she had yelled at and commended her. The clerk quickly regained her composure and we were all proud to be working for a manager that would stand up for his employees. Finally, after she had left, all the customers broke out in applause and thanked the manager for his fine job on throwing her out!

As a side note to that story, that same customer returned to shopping at our store about a year later after being thrown out of another chain store, and by then, she had improved her manners considerably! I was fairly impressed with the way that manager handled situations, because he spoke and did what was necessary, no matter the consequences. Of course, that was back when you could actually speak the truth to somebody without them suing you blind and having you fired.

As we are going about our work, it would seem to the usual patron that bagging groceries is a simple, straight forward job. On the contrary, you can never do it right. What you think is the sensible way to pack the bags for one person can seem atrocious to the other. One customer will bark, "You're making the bags too heavy!, and the next will say, "Stuff those bags full, we need to save the planet." When the choice was limited to large, medium, and small paper bags, the trick was to fill the bag without having it rip. Then came the coined phrase, "paper or plastic?" Plastic was cheap and it had handles, and so the tide eventually shifted to plastic. Plastic has its own problems in that it doesn't keep its shape. If you've ever put your plastic bags in the back of a pickup truck, you know that it is like tossing everything into a tumbler. These days, however, ecological issues have arisen, and the price of oil makes plastic bags a point of contention. "Would you like plastic bags?", we ask, and we get the reply, "How dare you jest!" So, you think that you have worked things out, and you ask the next customer, "Would you like paper bags?", and they reply, "How am I supposed to get those things up three flights of stairs?" Now we ask, "Would you like an ecologically friendly, re-usable bag made out of recycled plastic bags?" Ooohhh!

After getting past that issue, we start loading up the bags. They are too heavy! You're using too many bags! Where are my eggs? Don't squish my bread. Double bag everything. I want paper inside of plastic. Don't put the meat with the produce. Throw it all in one bag. You see the dilemma. What works for one person, won't work for the next. There is a guy that comes in and says, "I want everything in two paper bags, not doubled." Every time he comes in, he buys a little bit more. The bags are so full and heavy, that if you breathe on them, they will burst. Many times it does, which makes me wonder, if the bags are going to rip, and we have to re-do it all, shouldn't we just double them in the first place? Nope, can't do it. That's not how he wants it, two paper bags, not doubled.

Having people bring in their own bags or use the new ecological bags is good, when they remember to bring them. However, people fail to take into consideration their optimism towards shopping. "I just came in for one thing", they always say. So, they just bring in one or two recycled bags. After coming up front with half a cart of groceries, we ask if they would like paper or plastic bags, and they reply, "No, just stuff it all in there." So, after getting ripped for squishing one person's food, we are then asked to purposely squish it all in there, and we watch them try to lift these bags out of the store without slipping a disk. Need help? No....O.k, off you go. On the other hand, we are now developing our new shoveling technique. Increasing numbers of people get up to the front and then moan, "I left my bags in the car". So, they advise us to just shove everything back into the cart after I ring them up and they will bag it themselves outside.

In addition to the 20 questions that have become standard, we also have these charity events that we are continually schlepping. You know, charity is good, and what began as a program to support "Jerry's kids" has turned into a constant barrage of whiners with their hands out. The smell of cash always captures attention, and so there is a line of moochers a mile long waiting to be the next charity to shake loose our customer's spare change. That is in addition to the gauntlet waiting outside. The managers no longer care about selling groceries and customer service, now they just yell at me, because I'm not selling enough of the charity banners that make them look good to their bosses. Earlier this week, they just screwed in a permanent donation box to our countertop that has a removable logo card, so that we will constantly be collecting money, and they just change the recipient by changing the card. I don't know. I just remember when my job used to involve selling groceries. Now, it seems that I am just a telethon volunteer.

Speaking of "Customer Service", we used to have a nice counter, where you could get special service or request an odd item or something like that. Eventually, it just turned into a return and complaint counter. Here is where things get interesting, because you find that the most amazing incidents of people's disregard and lack of respect comes in the form of returns. You have never heard such stories, or seen such a sorry display, than when you stand there and listen to the song and dance people do, when they want to return something. We've since deleted the customer service counter....we were the ones getting serviced.

Nowadays, people come up to return bad milk, a bad melon or something, so you tell them fine, get yourself another one or we'll refund your money, whatever you like. Then they just stand there like "Guido" and say, "Hey.... what's in it for me? I had to drive all this way back to the store, burn my gasoline, and waste precious minutes of my life." Now they want to claim damages including pain and suffering. They want compensation. "What did you have in mind, exactly?" Well, let's see. How about free food for life, a new car, a vacation house in Hawaii.....etc. That's when I put the kibosh on them. If they ask for ridiculous stuff, then they get nothing! If they are reasonable, then I have something to work with.

Well, this manager I spoke of earlier confronted a woman concerning her frequent returns one day. At the time, we had a policy of double your money back if you were dissatisfied with the meats that you purchased at the store. So, although it works great for advertising, it also indulges some of those, who would take an entrepreneurial attitude toward such a policy. This particular woman would buy a large steak, eat half of it, then bring the other half back and say she didn't like it and wanted double her money back. Fair enough. However, after telling that same story a few times, and then buying the same thing again, the manager told her she was cut off. He said, "If you don't like our steaks, then go down the street and buy them somewhere else."

This happens quite often, believe it or not. People often buy things at sale price, then try to return it at full price making a small profit. It is such a petty thing and the amounts are not exactly exuberant in a grocery store. It seems to me, that some just enjoy trying to get something out of you. You just want to slap them on their hands with a ruler, but you'll get thrown in jail for that kind of thing these days.

Speaking of returns, just the other day, a lady came through the express lane with a return. "I need to return this", she says. "Alright", I say, as I proceeded to post the virtual stop sign to the other customers in line. "Do you have a receipt?", I ask. "Sure do", she says, and she proceeds to provide it to me. I notice that the paper has faded to browns and yellows and the print has just about worn off. So, in an inquisitive manner, I tell her, "It would seem that this was purchased in January." "Yes", she replies with a smile. I look down and then up again. "This is September.", I note. It made no nevermind to her.

She proceeded to tell me that it is her mother's item, and she is currently out visiting from back east, and she is doing this as a favor for her mother. All very true, I'm sure, but do you mean to tell me that this has been sitting around for nine months and your mother just waits for you to come 3000 miles in order to return it for her? I think to myself. Can she find no use for this item in all that time? Doesn't anybody else tend to her during the nine months you are gone? I wish I could actually speak all these questions and more that come to mind as I try to put together the reasoning behind it all. But thinking about it only makes it worse. So off she went with her refund. At least she had a receipt.

You know, most things people return cannot be put back on the shelf, so it just gets thrown away. In all decency, we can't knowingly sell food items that have been in other people's dirty hands and homes to other customers. It is just money that gets thrown in the garbage and then increases the cost of other items in the store. Here are some of my favorites:

Common ones: A lady brings back her meats and wants a refund because all of her meats were bad and stinky. However, somewhere in the conversation, she happens to let it slip that after shopping at our store, she went to a large discount shopping center for a few hours. So, I asked her if she felt that it might be possible that her meats went bad, while sitting in the trunk of her car in the summer heat while she shopped elsewhere? "Nope", she replied, we just sold her bad meat. So, off she went with her refund.

"I would like to return these and here is my receipt." "O.k., no problem. Ma'am, do you know why all of these cans are hot?" "Well, I put them in my car the other day, but I wasn't able to make it to the store until today." So, what you are trying to tell me, is that you don't want them anymore, so you want your money back, but we can't sell them to anyone or even give them back to you to eat, because you have ruined them by cooking them in the heat of your car for days, and you want us to take the loss and not you? This is what I really wanted to say, but of course it didn't come out that way, and off she went with her refund.

I could go on like this for years, but here is my favorite one. This one tops the cake for disregarding any respect for dignity or decency. It is even a bit morbid.

One day, a man steps up and says he wants to return a few items. So, he proceeds to pull out half a dozen condiments that had been unused. He had a ketchup, a large jar of Grey Poupon, a bottle of salad dressing, etc. I asked him if he had a receipt, and he said no. He told me, that they were his father's, and that his father had always shopped here. "O.k.", I said. I noticed that the labels had yellowed and so I began to look over the items and let him know that these items were pretty old. A couple of them were expired and one of them was old enough, so that the labels had since been updated to a new design. So, I inquired about them further, and so he finally told me the whole story. His father had died, and he was returning these items, because they were unopened.

WHAT???!!! (Blowing my top internally) You mean to tell me, that your father has died, and all you can think about is to return his ketchup and mustard for a whopping total of about six dollars? Then, you want me to put this nasty old expired stuff back on the shelf and sell the remaining condiments of a deceased man to somebody else? Are you out of your mind? What kind of person are you? Did your father raise you to be this sick of an individual? These and much more were the thoughts and questions I had raised behind my calm and pleasant demeanor. Even at that moment, I knew that this one topped the cake! How sick can you get?

A typical scenario: I need to return these items. "O.k., do you have a receipt?" "No, but I only shop here". "Well, ma'am, a couple of these items we don't carry in our store, and these ones have the competitor's logo on it". "No, I definitely bought them here, I don't shop anywhere else!" "I see". "Well, why would we be selling the store brand products of our competitor?" "I don't know, I just want to return them."

An eyebrow raiser: "Diapers, baby food, baby formula, wipes, are you buying these items?" "No, I want to return all of them." "Do you have a receipt?" "No, but I only shop here." "Of course, but why are you returning all of these?" "Well, the baby has grown and doesn't need any of these anymore." "I see." Off she went with her refund, and into the garbage it all went. All had been well baked in her car, of course. Then I thought, who in their right mind would want to shop knowing that they were buying second hand baby food? I wonder what that same customer would have thought if she new that we had taken back old baby food and goods from someone else and tried to resell it to her? Exactly!

Why don't people just use the things they buy? Sorry, I have no answer for that. It must be one of those sociological disorder things.

Meanwhile, I am back in the express lane and along comes another of my favorites, the ad shopper. Now the ad shopper can tell you every detail of the ad. They go over it with a microscope. They can tell you where in the world the paper was made and even the serial number of the ink dye that was used in the printing, but for the life of me, they cannot read the large print that says when the ad begins and ends. You see the numbers and letters there? That says Saturday, the fourth. Today is Wednesday, the first....

Now mind you, there is a bit of understanding on our part. The stores set up this maze with all the little games and coupons in their ads in order to confuse the customers on purpose. Not that their intent is to upset anyone, but the bosses feel that all this nonsense makes the store more mysteriously appealing, and sets us apart from the other stores. It doesn't really work. It simply stems anger and discontent, and leaves me standing there trying to explain it all and suffer the retribution. But, as I tend to point out, this is the work that results from having silly little nerds boxed up in cubicles in front of a computer screen and strobing them with fluorescent lighting all day. Truthfully, everyone seems to accept that as a viable answer. I believe it. I think a lot of the problems in humanity are the result of fluorescent lighting. It wierds me out after a little while too. Can't you tell? Did you ever see the beginning of that Tom Hanks movie, "Joe Versus the Volcano"? You know what I mean? It really would explain a great deal of the insanity.

So, last week, I am there ringing up three items for a lady. "Wait", she says. How much are you charging me for that jelly? It is supposed to be on sale! It is right there in your ad." "Well, let's open up the ad together and take a look. Uh huh, it says right here that this sale begins on Sunday. This is Saturday". Then, after careful review and a bit of moaning and groaning, she tells me, "I drove 20 miles to get here, and I'm not going to come back until next week. Can't you give it to me for that price today?" "Nope", I reply. Like old faithful, I could sense my favorite line come bubbling forth. "Where's the manager?" She says. I pointed her to the nearest pawn, but after wandering about the store and pleading her case to three different managers, she returns and tells me she wont pay the extra $1.10 and to take the jar of jelly off of her order. So much for the express lane, the other customers and I were all twiddling the entire time.

While I was waiting for that certain event to play out, my line had increased considerably, and I was happy to be able to move on to the next customer, who had giggled with me about the proceeding customer. Then she hands me her item and says, "I would like to return this." We giggle some more, and she hands me a receipt from six months earlier, to retrieve her grand total of $1.99 plus tax! It was one of those days.

We often have coupon specials in our ad, where you have to clip out the coupon to receive the discount on a sale item. Many don't bother cutting out the coupons anymore, they just shove the ad to us not wanting to bother with it saying, "The coupon is in there." Now, these particular coupons are supposed to be, "one per customer". So then is created the coupon cheater, which also resembles the express lane cheater. Let me explain.

These are the ones, who while trying to cheat the system to beat the system, just add to the misery. What they do is so obvious, that they think that nobody will notice. The express lane cheater will have too many items, so they will put some of the items on one order, and then put down a divider. Then, they place the rest of their items on a second or third order. So, each order is less than 10 items, but they have many orders. This one is for my mother, or this one is for my daughter, or grandma, uncle, aunt, cousin, through the whole family lineage. The coupon cheater wants to buy more than the allowed amount, so they put some on one order, and place a divider. Then, they place some on another order and so forth using the same excuses as the express cheater, all of which detracts from the concept of "express" and gets me into trouble with either the management or the customers. You can't win. You just have to decide who would you rather have yell at you today, the customer or the boss.

Moving back to business, we occasionally, or in some areas, regularly, get the perpetual governmental dependants. The government has programs that are well intentioned to assist those in need, but like anything else, are just ripe with abusers. There are food stamp cards that many use, and then there are WIC checks, which are vouchers that specify what food items and baby formulas you may purchase. Some of these things just take ungodly amounts of time to use, and we are constantly reminded that if we make any procedural errors, CSI will track us down and call in backup to have us hogtied and carried away for our flagrant violations and fraudulent abuse of government funds. Who would have ever thought that this job carried such national importance.

Uh, oh, here she comes. She gets in line with children coming out of every orifice. You simply want to tell her to put a cork in it, already! She hands us her WIC vouchers as she tries to keep her squad corralled. You want to feel bad for her and hope the government program will help. But the fact remains that she was on the program two years ago and two children ago, and she couldn't afford the kids she had then, and now there are more? To top it off, she brings up the wrong items on the vouchers. She doesn't care if we get fired. I mean, it would only seem decent, that if you are getting the food for free, that you might pay attention concerning how to use the program and to pick up the correct items. No, that's not how things work. Oh, mister bagger, can you take these items back and get the right things for me please? All you can do is shake your head. Needless to say, it irks me all the more, when I have to peek upwards, in hopes that their eyes might also notice the tarnished reputation of the express lane sign. Sorry, I am ranting.

There are many people that use the governmental assistance to help them during a bad time. They show an appreciation for the program and make efforts to move on. But sad to say, many people make it a lifestyle to use and abuse the system and continue to produce children they cannot afford. They just have such disrespect for themselves and the people around them, purposely freeloading off the system. You just look at the cute little kids and hope that it doesn't become an inherited trait. Well, you have to just shake it off, and move on to the next customer.

Meanwhile, back at the ranch, due to experience and training, I tend to be quicker than most, and when I am checking at a regular checkstand, some customers comment on the speed at which I move them along. So I reply to them, "If you want to wait around, you have to get into the express lane!" Yep, the concept of the "express lane" has just about outlived its usefulness. I have seen slow fast lanes, fast slow lanes, and some that are simply stagnant. The difficulty in accepting it all, is not just that people are in more of a hurry than they used to be, but that management has the ability to relieve much of this anxiety, but their thinking is likened to the casinos, in that, the longer they keep you in the store, the odds favor the house. The longer you wait in line, the more you buy. The Snickers and Reese's start to look pretty tasty, and the mental junk food in the latest tabloids about celebrity cellulite, will occupy that void in your life long enough for you to get through it.

Ahhh, it is finally time for my break. It may not seem like it from the other side of the counter, but working in the checkstand takes quite a toll on your body. You get stiff standing there all day, and your fingers and arms take a bit of punishment. So, when your break arrives, you try to squeeze the most out of it, before the next rush arrives. You have to be careful about saying "break" out loud, because as soon as you do, people sense it and come rushing up to the front to be checked out. At our job, you can't just leave to use the restroom whenever you want, you have to call someone to replace you. So, you just have to try to slip away when you can.

At one of the stores where I was working, there is a stairway that leads to the office and break room upstairs. (Sidepoint) I noticed that there are extra wide halls, doors, and stalls in the restrooms upstairs for the handicapped. However, there is no elevator. So, in reality, a handicapped individual in a wheelchair would have to roll to the bottom of the stairs, crawl up the stairs dragging his wheelchair up the full flight, hop back in his chair, and then proceed to wheel himself into the nice, extra wide restroom stalls! And you thought the craziness was limited to the checkstand. Not to worry, there are handicapped restrooms downstairs too. In addition, I don't know if any of you have noticed also, but all the bathroom facilities keep getting lower to the ground. I'm not getting any taller, so I know it's not me, but each time we get a new fixture or paper holder, they keep mounting it lower than before. I inquired about it once, and they told me it was to accommodate the handicap regulations. But honestly, and I am not kidding, in our current bathroom stalls, even "mini-me" would have to bend down to get the toilet paper out of our fancy dispensers, that are inches above the floor, and I almost have to kneel to use the urinal!

Meanwhile, upstairs in the office and breakroom, there are 2-way mirrored glass windows, so that you can view most of the store from upstairs. It was probably installed for security purposes, but when you are there on your break looking through the windows, it's like watching t.v. You look down one aisle, and there is domestic violence and verbal abuse. You look off to the left, and you can see theft in progress. Look off to the right, and there are smoochers waltzing down lovers lane. It is mesmerizing. One day I was peering through the glass while eating my lunch, and I hear a crash. I looked up the aisle to see a woman who was not watching where she was going while pushing her cart, and she ran into a display of coffee mugs sending many of them crashing to the floor. She was startled for a moment.

She looked ahead, then behind, then left and right down the center aisle, and she noticed that nobody saw her do it. So, she high tailed it down the aisle pushing her cart as quickly as she could to get out of there! Seeing the whole thing, I couldn't resist. So, I quickly grabbed the "com" line and announced over the loud speaker, "Clean up on aisle number 12!!" She double timed it out of there.

Ohhh my, the driving, and you thought it was bad at the DMV. Now mind you, many of the carts don't exactly go straight down the aisle, but if you could only watch how people steer these things, you wonder how it is that they even made it to the store, knowing that they drove here in an automobile! I don't think I want to go outside anymore. People of all ages bump, knock around, and bowl everything over. It's like a bumper car arcade, which is now a reality, by the way.

We now have what is called the "mart cart", which is just a fancy name for a bumper car. Now that people, especially the elderly, are riding around in these things instead of pushing a cart, there is real destruction taking place. Not only do the store and the merchandise take a beating, but there is a bit of indoor hit and run too! We're going to have to start selling insurance for driving these things, or call in the "mall cop" on a Segway.

One customer we have drives what could only be described as a 4X4 go cart. It is a mobility scooter that is bigger than my Mini Cooper. It could crush a "Rascal" as if it were in a monster truck rally. She drives this thing on the street in the bike lane at a pretty good rate of speed and has one of those tall dune buggy flags attached. Anyway, whenever she comes barreling through the checkstand, she always gives the counter and magazine racks a good whack. She backs up and then hits the gas again....Whack! Backs up, and then tries again, saying, "I know it fits, I have squeezed through here before...."Whack! What she really needs is side and rear view mirrors to see all the people she treads over every time she backs up.

Despite the dangers, customers always want to break the rules and take the mart carts outside for a cruise. We even get phone calls from some, who can't or won't bother to walk inside the store. They want valet service, so they call on their cell phone and say, "Have one of those kids bring a mart cart out to me. I'm sitting in a white car out in the parking lot". Then watching them try to maneuver between parked and moving cars, I have to cover my eyes. Look out, it's Mr Magoo, "....Oohh, I've done it again."

As you watch the demolition derby, you have to guard your tongue not to speak the thoughts that come to you. One extremely large gentleman waives two of us over to him while he was beginning his shopping using the mart cart. So he says to us, "This cart is moving really slow. I think there is something wrong with it". The other employee and I kind of look at each other with large eyes knowing that the man must weigh in at about 400 pounds with rolls of fat folding over the armrests of the seat. We reply to him that we don't know what's wrong with the cart, it worked fine earlier. In reality however, I mumble to myself that, it's because the cart has a 1 ton limit! Sorry, it's mean, but I couldn't help thinking that, because even the rubber wheels were squishing under the weight. One size does not fit all.

I keep saying that we are going to have to get trailers for those things, because it's amazing to see just how much stuff people pile all over the mart cart and themselves. They look like a float in the Rose Parade, when some of them roll up to the front check out. I keep waiting to see if the thing is going to tip over one day.

The lure of the mart cart is also strong amongst the teen crowd. Often, we have to kick off teenagers, who are cruising through the store on a joy ride. "Those are for handicapped or injured persons", I say, and then I wait to see what sort of sickness or injury they pretend to have.

There was a group of teenagers that would come in almost every night. They would wait until we were busy. Then, they would take the mart carts out to race in the parking lot or throughout the store. We would always get word from some customer saying that there are kids that just about ran them down playing with the mart carts. Then, they got the big idea that they should stack the cereal boxes like a brick wall on the aisle and then plow through them with the mart carts! This became a regular occurrence, and when we went to catch them, they would always bolt out the door. So, one evening, one of our baggers caught them making their mess. She ran after them yelling at them saying, "I'm the one who has to clean up that mess you make every night…..I'm going to get you!!" She was pretty fast, and she caught one of them outside in the parking lot and started beating on him. We had to go out there get her off of him. Suffice to say, the occurrence of this behavior diminished after that.

Now, while shopping, many people like to snack as they shop. My father used to do that regularly. For some, they are just starved, due to their busy life, but for many, their children just need a little something to keep from aggravating their parents into a fury. Awhile back, the Hostess company came up with a new cupcake called Dino Bites. They were Hostess cupcakes that were decorated in various colors and were shaped with teeth marks on the edge to make it look like a dinosaur had taken a bite out of it.

They were on sale one week, so a nice mother conceded to her two young boys and chose to buy a package. Now, one of the boys was old enough to walk beside the cart, but the other was sitting in the child seat. The mother decided to give the boys a treat, so she popped open the package and gave a cupcake to each one of them. However, the little boy in the seat through his hands in the air and started yelling, "Aaaahhhh, I don't want that one, Aaaahhhh!!!" So, the mother put that one back and picked out another to hand to the little boy. "Aaaaahhhhh, I don't want that one either, Aaaaahhhhh!!!" So, once again, the mother put that one back and tried another but with the same result. It turns out that the little boy thought that his older brother had taken a bite out of each one and didn't like them, so he was not going to eat them either! Kids are funny. Meanwhile, the sale of Dino Bites didn't last very long. As another fellow employee commented, "Who wants to pay full price for cupcake with one less bite in it?"

As I mentioned before, the store is really like a second home for most people, so the children feel free to play and horse around, and so it becomes like a playground. Then when the parents are done shopping, they come up front and ask us to call their children over the loudspeaker, like ringing the bell for dinner.

One family in particular happened to be quite a nuisance. I would also classify them amongst the moochers that graze about the store. There are some that would like to "try before you buy". Then there are those who have no intention of purchasing any of the things that they are munching on. So, when this particular family would arrive in the store, we would just let out a sigh, "Oh no, here we go again". They had a handful of kids that would just tear off down the aisles in all different directions as soon as they entered the store. While the parents would shop, the kids would open up toy packages, eat out of the candy bins, munch on various produce items, same as their parents of course, and throw the evidence about the store.

So, one day, one of the employees decided to confront the parents and said, "Do you know that your kids are eating everything in our store and tearing open packages without paying for them?" The parents looked back at the employee with the blank look of a bovine, and said, "So what?" The employee tried to express to them that this was unacceptable behavior and a loss to the store and so forth, but to no avail.

It was then that I realized the professional work of the petty thief. When someone steals something that is only worth a couple bucks, it's not worth it to the store or to the police to do anything about it. It costs too much labor and paperwork to make it worthwhile, and there is a certain level of society that takes advantage of that fact. But I also realized that this is the sort of people who don't monitor their expenses. So although it is a bit unethical, we would just simply add those items that they ate onto their order, unbeknownst to them, while we rang up the rest of their items.

A similar experience came about on a busy day. One of the employees came up to me at the checkstand and said, "Do you see that man at the end of the line? Well, I saw him order a bag of fried chicken at the deli counter. He ate the chicken while he was shopping, then he threw the chicken bones and the bag onto the shelf on one of the aisles. He then went back to the deli and told them that he had misplaced his chicken and needed another bag full!" "I'll take care of it", I told her. Noticing that the man was large and gruff, I decided not to get into a "yes you did, no I didn't" argument in front of everybody, so I simply greeted him nicely and proceeded to add an extra bag of chicken to his order without mentioning it. Then as I predicted, he paid his bill, thanked me, and told me he did not need his receipt. I hate to have to resort to this sort of thing, but the checkstand is not the greatest place to address bad behavior, despite the entertainment value.

Fighting with the customers never makes you look good. Although I am told by my bosses to take the next customer in line, I seldom do so, because sometimes the fair thing to do is not the right thing to do. I usually just walk up front and let the customers in line know I am opening up. That way, the obnoxious pushy people will jump at the opportunity, and I can get rid of them quickly. Many times, the person in the front of the line has a full basket, and the person behind them just has a handful, so I offer the latter the chance to scoot ahead of persons, who would otherwise make them wait behind their full basket of groceries with coupons and checks and such.

I base my decision partly on an event I saw awhile back, when the assistant manager opened up an empty checkstand. He went over to a little old lady, who was the next in line to the left. Meanwhile, a gentleman who was next in line to the right with just a couple items came up to the same newly opened checkstand. As the assistant manager took his place behind the register, he noticed that the man was there, and told him that he would have to wait, because the little old lady was next in line. So, the man mentioned that he was next in line in the other lane. So, the argument began and escalated into a fistfight! Watching the whole thing take place, I said to myself, "That wasn't very bright." The assistant manager could have checked out the man and had him on his way, before the little old lady even emptied her basket! Instead, he got into a fight and made himself look like an idiot. He alienated a customer, who will probably never shop here again, and he lost a sale. Sacrilege! So, I myself simply let the customers flow as they should. Let the pushies push their way out, so that I can spend more time and give better service to the well behaved.

Sometimes too, the nice customers have habits that are cute to watch, because they have such a pleasant demeanor, but difficult to deal with when there are dirty looks coming from buzzing hornets in line behind them waiting to get out.

Times are not like they used to be, and watching someone balancing their checkbook after casually writing me a check in the express lane just doesn't sit well with people anymore. May I see your I.D.? "Wait just a moment, while I write all this down or else I will forget." Sure….(whistling interlude).

There is one habit, which is a worldwide phenomenon. I haven't quite narrowed down what causes it, but it begins when a woman says, "I have the exact change." Stop the press! I have no idea what gene it is, that makes women feel the need to give the exact change. In the end, it all adds up to the same amount anyway! So, what difference does it make? Many a husband tries to make this same point, but there is nothing that can persuade women otherwise. It always makes me smile, when this occurs, because there is nothing you can do but sit back and wait.

Down they go, diving into the bottomless pit of their purses, pulling out all the flotsam and jetsam accumulated therein, setting it on the counter in order to dig up the dirty change that has shaken its way down to the bottom. The little coin purse just doesn't have enough, so she checks her purse again.

No, she won't give me the nickel, because she has five pennies that she wants to get rid of. Then she starts to check her pockets and then asks everyone accompanying her if they have any change on them. It is a sick disease with no cure. She will hold up everyone in the store and essentially stop the world from turning until she gets every last penny. It's amazing. Then, when she finally gets that last coin and hands it to me, she is pleasurably ecstatic, almost orgasmic in happiness, and I'm only glad to have obliged. Of course, if they don't arrive at the exact change, they look dejected. They look up at me as if they just failed all womankind, and I assure them that everything will work out just fine. Amidst all that, a boyfriend can apply subterfuge and slip me an extra dollar to cover the amount and then receive change and get away with it. But if a husband tries the same, the wife, with her hands still in her purse growls and gives him the look of death sending him the signal that says, he gets no dinner or "dessert" tonight, if he foils her attempt to make change!

O.k., the total for all your goodies is $68.95, "What a deal". "Would you like me to help you with that?" "No, I can do it." One of the types of customers that I enjoy toying with is the "germaphobe". You should see the un-delicate ballet of the person, who tries to be part of society, but does not want to touch anything! These days, we now have sanitary wipes as you walk in the door in order to wipe your hands and the handlebars on the carts. Some, however, are the extremists. They carry a slew of wipes with them throughout the store, and then finally hands the wad to me at the checkstand. Oh, like I want to touch them now! My favorite is watching them do their silent facial eeeeekk, when they look at the ATM pin pad, calculating to themselves how many people have touched that thing today, and yesterday, and the day before, knowing that it is brimming with bacterial activity. Some use the edge of their card to touch the keys, and some use a pencil, pen, or some other object. As they wiggle their way through the miniscule minefield, they are relieved in a way, because they couldn't bear the thought of touching cash. Granted, there are still those, that lick their fingers as they count their cash, and who knows how many bras the bills have padded, but there is generally a simple rule. Keep your hands out of your mouth, and wash before you eat. As the transaction has completed, the "germaphobe" feels so icky, that they need to wash up, so off to the restroom they go trying to turn the door handle with their elbows. Yes, I know, the bigger the microscope they make, the more germs they find, but you really can't live your life like that. It's not good for the kids either. Kids need dirt.

We have a relatively new bagger, who is growing up to be just this sort of person. He is only 17 right now, and he wears gloves with a rubber coating on them while he is working. That is not completely demented, but then the other day, I caught him using the hand sanitizer. He was not putting it on his hands like a normal individual, he was putting it all over his rubber gloves! I commented on his odd behavior, and told him that he needs to start therapy right away, before he grows up to be "bubble boy"!

Meanwhile, there are many different ways to hold up the line, many of which I have already mentioned, but there is a new one that is growing by leaps and bounds. This one I partially understand, because due to the decreasing competency of the workforce being hired, people find it frustrating not to be able to find or get the items they came for. In the past, people would ask an employee who is working on the floor to help them find or retrieve items before they come up to the front. Now, many people stake their claim to their spot in line, scatter their goods upon the checkstand, and then run off to do more shopping. Or, after ringing up all of their goods and giving them a total, they ask me, "Can you have somebody check in the back to see if you have any more of this?" Or, "I couldn't find these items, can you get them for me?" "Fine, and I assume you want me to tell everybody else, that they can just wait all day until we get you what you want?" I grumble to myself. "Why didn't you ask, before you got in line?" I always wonder. Personally, I think people enjoy making others wait for them. It's a display of empowerment. So, in extreme cases, I apply the concept they use in the drive through at some of the fast food joints. Just go park over there, so we can get on with things until we are done with you.

Here is one I watched the other day. Two people walked up to the express lane at the same time. There was one nice lady with three or four items in her hands, and one younger kid, who beat her by one step. Instead of letting her go first, he stood there, holding her at bay, while he summoned his siblings and his mother, who was pushing a cart no less, and escorted them in first. They had more than the allotted items in their basket, of course. I rang up their stuff as quickly as I could, but to no avail. After finishing her phone conversation, the mother seemed rushed and flustered, and you could see it in her face that her mind was elsewhere, meditating on the finished conversation and trying to think if she got everything she needed. Then, how did I guess? She pulls out her checkbook. (Naptime intermission) Finally after giving them the figurative "boot" and the bad manners award for the day, I commented to the next fine lady on her wonderful patience.

It is all these little things that add up. Each of which drives you further toward insanity. As I try to sort out each one, they continue to pile up more, so that all your effort still makes it seem like you're moving in mud. But, I keep trudging along.

Now, I don't know whether it's because people are becoming more addicted to gambling, or maybe it's the end result of the grown up video game junkies, but there are more beeps, blips and doinks than ever before. Even the new ATM they just installed at the bank in our store sounds like a slot machine. Now whenever an item doesn't scan, the register gives out a certain beep, and immediately the customer throws up their hands and yells, "It's free!" Any strange sounding beeps seem to inspire a euphoric reaction, like they just hit the jackpot. The oddity is in the fact, that everyone has that same reaction. They all say the same thing, "It's free!" Something for nothing, isn't that what everyone is trying to achieve these days? Sorry, you crapped out. Price check....

Finally, everything is scanning smoothly, and things are moving right along, so I look around to view the scene. Observing the latest fashion is always enjoyable. We get everybody in every sort of clothing parading into the store. There are those that are dressed for summer, who then freeze as they come shopping inside. They ask me why it is so cold in the store? So, I reply that it is to keep our chocolate bars from melting. There are some that wear the same clothes over and over, and not just for work. There are some, who haven't showered in years and make my eyes water. They reach into their pockets and hand me a pile of money. I look at it wondering if I should send it to the lab for testing or something. I feel that I need a shower after they walk by. At least I'm awake now. Their sent works like smelling salts! I just wish that they would stay downwind.

The other night a scroungy looking guy came through. He resembled George Carlin and was wearing a dirty trench-coat. His appearance was that of the dumpster divers we get out back. So, what was he buying? Crest Whitestrips! Those aren't cheap, either. So, I had to give him a good second looking over. Maybe I was missing out on the latest urban dumpster fashionista or something. Nope. He was simply an unkempt guy, who wanted to make sure he has a nice bright smile! Weird.

Oh man! Last night, I could smell this guy before he even came near. He stank and was covered in white flakes. He was just snowing with dandruff. I have some understanding for the 100 year old guy, who can't get in and out of the shower without help, but this guy wasn't old or disabled. To top it off, he comes strolling through my line, blabbing away on his cell phone! I mean, who is this, Howard Hughes? He doesn't shower, but he has enough friends, so that he is on the cell phone all day? If you can afford a cell phone, you can afford a bath. Where we live, there is just no excuse. We're near the beach, and there are free showers right there. Take a dunk in the ocean, while you are at it, and let the fish nip you clean, why don't ya'.

We had a regular customer, who would do just that. I guess you could say he was homeless, because he did live on the street. But he was a clean and responsible adult. After a bit of curiosity, we finally got his story. He had fallen on bad times. So, he slept on bus benches, and would carry two suitcases with him everywhere. He would use public restrooms to keep clean and shaven, and he had a job at a local taco shop. He would come in almost every morning with his two suitcases and get a little something for breakfast. To me, he is a pretty important guy. He shows that you can be down on you luck and living on the street, but still be a clean, decent, hard working person. You don't have to be a scumbag. So, if you are a dirty street scumbag, it is because you want to be, not because you have to be.

Speaking of fine fragrances, one middle aged woman got in line the other day and was unloading her cart, but she smelled like she needed a diaper change. Now mind you, the end of the checkstand is at least six feet away from where I stand, but still, my nose hairs were curling. When she finally came near and faced me, I realized that the smell wasn't her backside, it was her breath! I don't think she had brushed her teeth since Nixon. Woof!

Meanwhile, most people wear what is comfortable, despite appearances and smells. Some come in dressed to the hilt to see and be seen. It is like something you might see on some of the latest t.v. programs. You kind of hear a "sha boom, sha boom", as they sashay their cart down the aisle.

Of course, you then wonder, what's cookin' tonight?

The store where I first began working, was located in close proximity to the beach and to Jazzersize just down the street. Obviously, many women feeling freshly charged with endorphins and a nice tan would come in for a bite and to show off their wares.

Most of us were locals, and were used to it, but occasionally, we would get a new employee from elsewhere. One time, we got a new store manager, who transferred in from a nasty neighborhood far away. Like any new manager, he gave us the "old gipper" speech. Then, he tried to lead the team and concentrate on his work, but for the first couple months, he was simply a blubbering fool. He basically became the store greeter with a big smile on his face, just being inundated with eye candy. He eventually got through it and got back to work. Poor guy, the job can be rough.

Not all customers are as appealing. One older gentleman, who also rides around in the mart cart, has some issue with his shoulder. So, he goes everywhere and does his shopping with only half of his shirt on, meaning that one arm is in the shirt, and the rest is just hanging off of him leaving half of his body exposed. So, after floating on air and gliding on your tip toes with glittering Jazzersize angels, nothing squares your vision like a good dose of grey back hair and man-boobs. Don't you think?

The latest fashion is not only amongst the customers,

but the employees too. I joke that all the new young male employees can only work with one hand. They use one hand for working while they use the other to hold up their baggy pants! In the same manner, women have been doing that for years. One hand is used for shopping, and the other is a hook for their purse. Or, as they bend to get items or to unload their carts, they have to use one hand to hold their blouse, while they reach with their other hand. However, there is a new dilemma. Showing your crack in the back has always been a favorite amongst plumbers and other construction crawlers, but nowadays, girls are wearing their pants so low, that their crack is showing. Meanwhile, as they bend to get the items they want, they have one hand holding their top to limit exposure, and the other hand is holding up the back of their pants for the same reason. I figure that something's gotta' give eventually! Maybe I should lend a hand.

Etiquette seems to be whatever comes to mind for the day. There used to be some sort of unified way of presenting yourself in public. There is always the "no shoes, no shirt, no dice" rule, but now, we just wait and see what may present itself as people stride through the doors. It's almost like the story of "The emperor's new clothes", where the emperor believes he is walking in the height of fashion as he strolls down the street half naked, not realizing that he has been duped by his designers.

The same occurs, when we have certain gentlemen, who believe that they are improving their public appearance by wearing a "rug" that is as old as the shag carpet in my Volkswagen. They always have the same look on their face that asks, "Is this working"? Remember that spray on hair in a can that was supposed to hide the bald spot? Useful, I guess, however, as the bald spot increases, the effectiveness it may have once had decreases. Well, there is a customer, poor guy, that would seem to use a full can every time. It's horrible. To me, it looks like he marks the edges of his old hair line with masking tape, glues fiberglass or steel wool to his head and then uses a can of flat black spray paint! I just can't imagine that someone actually thinks that this looks better than the alternative. ....Note to readers, natural always looks best.

As people come through, I am always curious to see the latest fashion accessories. When I first became a checker, the punk scene was fairly new, and the wardrobe was not yet mainstream. Two guys came up to the counter buying a few things that included some studded dog collars. They had spiked hair and torn shirts, and so out of curiosity, I asked them, "You don't have dogs, do you?" "Nope", they said. So, off they went putting their new collars and chains around their neck and wrists.

There are all sorts of tattoos and piercings available to see, but one of the latest trends is the, Paris Hilton, I have to carry my dog everywhere accessory. Despite the fact that it is against the law to bring any animals into the store, due to the health department regulations, people never fail to brandish their lawlessness. There are, in rare instances, people who are actually blind and need their seeing eye dog, which is allowed, but everyone else is just tromping the rules.

First we have the whiner. She whines and cries, that, "There is no way that she could possibly leave her baby in the car." I cannot be without my little pookie for a minute or something bad might happen. The pooch just looks at me with those puppy dog eyes that say, "I just wish she would let me down for a minute so I can sniff around". Next we have the one that says, If I just hold my dog the whole time, then it's o.k. Sorry, it's not. By this time, however, everybody already knows that it is wrong, so they simply hide their dogs. Some have them hidden under their shirt, until the dog's head pops out from under their collar. Some have them hidden in their purses. Some just let them sit in the basket as if they are carrying their child.

Just last week, we were looking at a woman pushing her stroller, which always attracts all the moms passing by. Then, as the blanket is pulled back, the head of some mutt pops out! Well, I definitely can see the family resemblance. To me, this is strange behavior, and it has become kind of a sick obsession. I mean, I like my dog, but not like that!

But, now that the law has been trodden, it paves the way for the stampede of the rest of the animal kingdom to arrive. Here come the cats. Then comes the guy with the snake around his neck followed by the lady with the giant parrot and other birds perched upon her shoulder and the cart. Then finally, the one that I couldn't believe that I actually saw. One girl comes walking into the store, so non-chalantly, with her pet rat on her shoulder!! I had to say something, so I went up and said, "Excuse me, but you realize that we are trying to keep the rats out of the store. We don't need people bringing them into the store!" Her response was predictable. She gave me the look of disbelief that I would possibly question her about bringing her close companion shopping with her. She dismissed my objection and continued shopping. Where is the lady with the cat, I though to myself. These two need to meet!

Speaking of animals, I've got to tell you these ones:

Usually, when the trucks arrive in the back, most of the animals are dead and ready to be put out on the rack of the meat department. However, one day, I am pulling a load of firewood off of the truck, when a huge rat jumps right off of the top of the pallet and takes off down the hall, through the double doors, right onto the sales floor. It then runs right along the entire case of the meat counter and then ducked into a corner, with a couple of us chasing it all the way.

Needless to say, it was a little difficult explaining to the customers, who saw the rat run by, that it was a fresh new rat that just came off of the truck, and that the rodent was not a current resident.

One time, a truck pulls up and backs in at the dock. The driver said he had quite a bumpy ride. Then when the back door to the truck was opened, which was delivering seafood, the lobster boxes had fallen over and all the lobsters were running around the truck snapping their claws! It took a bit of dancing to collect them all again without getting pinched.

This story I love to tell every time I sell a large bag of dog food. One day, a tiny little old lady comes up to the front and says, "Can you have somebody help me put a 40 pound bag of dog food into my cart?" "Sure", I say. Then as I rang her up, she said, "Can you have somebody help me put the dog food into the trunk of my car?" "Sure, no problem". So, then I asked her, "How do you get that big bag of dog food out of your car, when you get home?" "I don't", she says. "When I feed the dog, I just open the trunk of my car, scoop out what I need, and then I close the trunk. Then, when the bag is empty, I throw it away and then buy another one." "You're a pretty smart lady", I told her, "But now I know why the dogs chase the cars down the street!"

You really do get to meet some intelligent and beautiful people, who have a lifetime of experience to share with you. Although I comment on some of the odd things that people do, they are all people just like you and me, sharing the best and the worst of themselves. When it comes to reading people, you can really tell a lot about them by the foods that they are buying. Obviously, the ones who can cook are buying gourmet type items to create an elaborate dish. However, beware of the spaghetti cook. I've come to know that if someone does not know how to cook, they always say that they make good spaghetti.

As I briefly say hello to all the customers I meet, I then take notice of the items they are purchasing as I continue with their order. There was a woman buying a bunch of ground turkey that was on sale. Ah, turkey burgers, I presume? She said, yes, and that she had been trying to get her family to eat healthier by using ground turkey instead of beef. She told me that she had been secretly using it when cooking, and the dinners were working out just fine. She told me that her husband looked into the freezer one day, and yelled, "What is this ground turkey doing in here? I'm not eating that!" She then proceeded to tell him that he had been eating it for the past few months, and he couldn't tell the difference! Pretty sly. So, the lesson is, if you are being fed and it tastes good, don't argue with the cook.

I always recall a certain incident that occurred with my old roommate, whenever I sell a stalk of anise or fennel. You see, he is one of those new age yuppies or granola heads that fall for all the latest, so-called, "healthy" food.

Of course, there is plenty of good food, that is actually healthy for you, and then there are all of those wonderfully strange products that advertise better health through modern scientific processing or by overloading the packaging with fancy words. For example, if there were two bags of beans on the shelf, and one of them says, beans for 99 cents, and the other says, Organic magic beans grown on the top of mountain cascades with little gypsies dancing all around for $3.99, my old roommate would pick the $3.99 bag thinking that they were somehow much healthier, when in reality, they are the same beans. You get the idea. Anyway, one day he comes home with some elaborate toothpaste that he paid too much for, and it was flavored with anise and fennel seed. Sounds amazingly healthy, doesn't it? Well, later that evening, I here an "aaaaauuuuugggghhhh"! "What was that?" I ask. "This toothpaste tastes like black licorice!!" "Yes", I told him. "Didn't you know what that stuff was, before you bought it?" "No", he replied, "It just sounded good".

Not to knock actual health food, but I have to mention a certain correlation that I have noted. There are all of those "healthy" meat replacement products that somehow turn soy beans and other goodies into fake meat. The pinnacle of which, has got to be the tofu hot dog, because the whole purpose of eating a hot dog is knowing that it is bad for you, but that it tastes good. So, having a healthy hot dog would defeat the whole purpose of eating a hot dog. But these days, it's better health through DuPont, I guess.

I worked at a store, where a number of the girls were vegetarian and would eat all of these strangely healthy products, and I have to say, they were always sick or not feeling good, and their color was a bit off. So, my conclusion is this: If you want to eat healthy, eat your fruits and vegetables, and if you want to pay extra money for fancy words, buy a book!

There are some things that people pay too much for, and it is simply a matter of culture. In our area, we sell plenty of menudo, beef tripe, or beef stomachs. I realize that many latinos use this to make a certain cultural dish, and I could see buying it if it were cheap, but you could buy a nice piece of steak or some chicken for the same price. I used to hate selling that stuff, because essentially, before it is cooked, it smells like it was washed in a dirty toilet! When people would purchase these items, the packages would drip all over my checkstand, and I would get it on my hands, and it would stink all over. After bagging it up, I would have to use the spray cleaner and mop up the mess.

Finally after finishing with that, the next customer would walk up and get a wiff of it. Then, they would then look up at me as if I just let one go, or wonder if I hadn't changed my underwear in a few months or something! When the smell finally abates, another customer always comes along with a fresh pack and plops it on the counter. Here we go again. Things are better nowadays. They finally got the hint, wised up, and started pre-packaging that stuff with a vacuum seal. Hooray!

There occasionally are odd moments like this, where the customer and the employee don't really speak their mind, because it would seem inappropriate. There are two instances, when the circumstance becomes a bit awkward, and there is a loss for further discussion. These both concern couples. The first, is when a couple comes through and are buying condoms, usually accompanied by some form of alcohol. I just look up at them and say in a glance, "What are you doing tonight?" The other is the couple that comes through buying an EPT test, wishing that they too had bought the condoms along with the alcohol. Trust me, it is nothing like the commercials that they show you on t.v. I just look up at them, and I see in their face, that they pretty much already know the answer, but buying the EPT test gives them the benefit of the doubt and just might offset their coming misery for a few more hours.

Following these is the man in trouble. Often we get a man buying flowers and a card, and we know that he is in big trouble with his wife or girlfriend, and so I always offer my support and say, "I hope it works"! The culmination of this scenario comes on Valentine's Day and Mother's Day. These are the only days of the year, where the male customers outnumber the female customers. The men are sifting through all the colorful items trying to remember what their girls like. They are so scared, but they are glad that they remembered to get something, because they know that if they show up home with nothing, they would be dead men! One man came up with a particularly disgusted look on his face buying flowers and candy, and he told me, that he actually did show up home with nothing, and his wife yelled at him and told him to get out of the house and not to come back home until he got her something! Now that's true love.

This is a good part about working at the store, knowing that we can help you in you time of need. Usually, your need is hunger, but sometimes you need something personal, like flowers and balloons, or something like that.

Being nosy is just part of the job. Our noses can be a little too big at times, however. If you didn't already know, you are being watched all the time. We ourselves, as curious employees, watch what it is that you buy, but there is also the "eye in the sky". Sometimes, it is to the benefit of the customers, but usually, it is for the benefit of the store. People will come back to the store and say, "I didn't get my twenty dollars cash back." Or, they might say, "The girl didn't give me all of my groceries." So, the boss goes into the office, looks at the video, and then comes out and tells the customer, "You put the twenty bucks into your jacket pocket." Then the customer sifts through their clothes, and says, "What do you know, there it is!" Or the boss might say, "On the video, the checkstand was clear. You received all of your bags, and you took your groceries outside and put them in your car. Where they are now, we don't know." It is good, I guess, but somehow, I think, it makes people a little uneasy.

Also, you may have noticed, that the computer is watching what you buy too. At certain stores, they can really monitor your behavior, but for the most part, there is a simple cause and effect in place. For instance, if you buy one brand of soda, then the computer might be programmed to spit out a coupon for a different brand of soda. Or, you might buy a salad, and you get a coupon for dressing. But lately, we've noticed that there might be a little too much imaginative thinking on the part of those trying to cash in on consumer purchases. One evening, a female employee purchased only one item, a jar of pickles. As I finished cashing out the order, the coupon machine sprang into action and printed up a coupon. She and I both looked at each other, because it seemed odd that the machine would churn out a coupon for such an unusual item. I then grabbed the freshly printed coupon and looked at it. I then showed it to her and we both laughed. It was a coupon for an EPT test! We both agreed that it was creative, but a little too far fetched, and possibly even a bit tasteless. I asked if she might be pregnant, and she looked at me as if to say, "Whatever", she not having any sort of male companionship at the time.

Sometimes, when you notice how people shop, you just have to ask, why? People, in general, are getting larger. Part of the problem is here at the store. We sell piles of junk food for cheap, and the healthy food will put you in hock. It used to be the other way around. But how you handle your girth is a whole different story.

I was watching a woman push her cart along, and sorry to say, she was carrying a few spare tires like the Michelin man. But what blew me away was when she would continue her shopping, she would grab a couple tires worth of her belly and plop it over the handle bar of the cart where it would jell and settle into the child seat area! Bbbbrrrrrr.... shivering and shaking my head! That's not right!

One family came through the line, and I said, "O.k. that will be 65 dollars." "I only have 40", he says. "Would you like me to take off the two cases of beer?" "No", he says, "Take off the Kool-Aid, ...and the cereal, uhmmm.... take off the bread". "Not enough" I said. "....uuuhhh, take off the baby food and the diapers". This went on until eventually, his family left the store with no food, just plenty of beer.

Sometimes you just want to intervene into the lives of people in order to help them understand the detriment of their behavior, but it's of no use. Much of what we see, are parents training their children in their own bad habits and ways. One mother and daughter would come through once a week buying the most enormous pile of junk food you could find. The mother was well over 300 pounds and the daughter was right in behind her. They were both wide enough, so that they had to walk through the checkstands sideways to squeeze through. Then when you rang up their groceries, they each would buy three 5 gallon tubs of ice cream, numerous bags of chips, cookies, frozen junk, fried foods, etc., just terrible stuff. It is a shame to think that her daughter never really had a chance. She grew up to be just like her mother.

You want to just grab them and say, don't do this to your children!! One mother we caught stealing, had stuffed her baby's stroller full of food all around the baby and covered it with a blanket, and then had her 4 year old stick hot dogs down his pants, and they all tried to walk out with it. "What are you teaching your kids?" You almost want to let them go, because they might need the food, but you can't let this kind of thing continue. You know what? The truth of the matter is, we have rarely caught anyone stealing, who didn't have the money to purchase the items they stole. They just steal for the heck of it. If someone were actually hungry and asked us if they could have some food because they have no money, we could definitely accommodate them with something.

Occasionally, even employees get busted for stealing from the store. We had a pharmacist working at my store, who was very friendly and helpful to the customers. He eventually got caught pilfering the medications he had behind the counter. To the rest of us, it was unfathomable, that someone who made over fifty bucks an hour would risk his job to steal pills! What? He needed the money? These days, you just never know whose hands are in the till.

Yes, theft is always a problem at the store. There are all kinds and all ages. It used to be, that when you caught somebody, you would take the item back and tell them not to come back to the store. Now, we receive the verbal flak in their staunch denial of said behavior. "How dare you accuse me of stealing, I would never do anything like that! Who do you think you are?" "Don't touch me or else I'll sue you for abuse." "My children would never do such a thing." "That was already mine, I bought it somewhere else." Well, you see where I'm going here. Ones caught red handed used to graciously admit their defeat, but now, even after telling them we have them on video, they still deny all charges against them, swearing upon every dead relative they have.

Meanwhile, there came a day when violent retaliation

became the final recourse. Go out fighting would seem to be the new motto. While chasing a guy running out the door with two 12 packs of beer, he realized that you can't run as fast with the extra weight, and that he would be caught. So, he stopped, dug in, ripped open the packages of beer bottles, and started launching them at us like grenades! While dodging the onslaught, one of the employees, who happened to be on the local football team charged him like a linebacker and sacked the offender. I wish I could have watched that one again on ESPN highlights. But it was then, that I noticed the change. If they couldn't keep the stolen merchandise, then they would destroy it. So, the games began.

It almost became sporting, as it were, catching a thief and retrieving the merchandise unharmed. There were those who were tackled, those who were hogtied, those that were billy clubbed, those that had their clothes torn off, received road rash, handcuffed, and so on. But then, it soon became apparent that they would stop at nothing in order to escape. They started pulling weapons. One employee got knifed in the hand, while trying to stop a guy from stealing a pack of cigarettes.

"You mean to tell me, that someone would send somebody to the hospital over a pack of cigarettes?" I thought to myself . So, the sport quickly faded away. Now, we have rules regarding the apprehending of thieves. It is no fun anymore. I realized, however, that if you confront somebody while they are still in the store, they are docile, but as soon as they reach the door, all hell breaks loose and it is every man for himself.

So, the art of prevention then came to light. You would figure that video would be a deterrent, but it really isn't. Those who want to steal will try their luck anyway. Some really give themselves away right off the bat.

Liquor is probably the most stolen item, due to its price and the fact that many teenagers want become alcoholics early in life instead of waiting until later. So, when we see youngsters wander straight in the door over to the liquor department, we usually follow them over. In addition to them are the rappin' ghetto stylers, who limp step their way over to the booze wearing giant heavy NFL style jackets in 90 degree heat. Gee, I wonder what they are up to? So, I developed a new strategy for all of these types. I would tell one of the young employees to follow them and stand 20 feet away from them and just smile. Follow them everywhere they go in the store staying 20 feet away, and if they ask you what you are doing, just tell them that your boss told you to do it. Quickly realizing that their cover is blown, they leave the store. It works!

Here are some good stories from the old days:

One of our older employees, who was raised in Texas,

waves me over to her counter. She looks at me and says, "You know, Scott, old people are the biggest crooks!" She told me about how she watched an old man walk over to the rack, pick out a pack of hearing aid batteries, then slip them into his shirt pocket. He then picked up a candy bar and went up to her counter to pay. She gives him that scornful southern look with the fists on the hips and asked him if he was also going to pay for those batteries in his pocket! "Oh, yes", he says, as he pulled them out of his shirt. "I'm getting old, and my memory is going." He said. She continued giving him the dirty look and said, "Well, I'm old too, and you don't fool me one bit!"

At some point every day, we walk through the store with a cart and collect all of the items that get strewn about, from people who change their minds while perusing the store. When we arrive at the section where we sell new shoes and sandals, we always stop for a moment to sift out the high mileage trade- ins. Yes, it happens regularly. People sidle up to the footwear, straddling on what suits them, then hang up their stinkers on the rack and swagger off!

One day, back when parachute pants were cool, a guy comes wandering out from the liquor aisle walking like a cowboy from the old west. Each bow legged step he took, you could hear this, ching, ching, ching, and he wasn't wear- ing spurs. So, the boss cuts him off before he walks out the door and says, "Do you want to give me those bottles you shoved down your pants, or shall I just push you over and let the glass break all over your legs?" So, the man reached in his pants and started to take out the bottles. We were quite amazed when he kept reaching in and pulling out bottles. Six bottles of wine he had stuffed down his pants! Nice try.

Of course, we had our regular thieves. They would come in every day or so and try to steal a 40 oz. bottle of beer. Sometimes we would catch them, sometimes not. No matter how many times we caught them, they would still come back again. The problem being, that it takes an hour's worth of paperwork to prosecute them and then have the police come take them away, only to let them go a short time later, because the beer is only $1.49. It isn't worth it to bust someone over such a small amount.

There were two guys in particular that really were a real nuisance. If we even saw them enter the store, we would throw them out. But they would always wait until we were busy and then sneak in. One of them we called the one-arm-bandit, because he had been in some sort of fire, and had burn scars and was missing part of one arm. That didn't keep him from using his good arm to rob us. He was a pain, because he would always give us an attitude like we were doing him some wrong for not letting him steal. Then once, during the dinner rush, the other pilferer snuck in and proceeded to get himself a beer and tried to walk right out the door. So, one of the managers, who was quite fed up with wasting time dealing with this guy so regularly, caught him, and walked him to the office in the back of the store. The guy was assuming that he would be doing the paperwork thing again. I happened to be right there, and so the manager tossed me the keys and told me to open the back door. So, I ran back and opened the back door.

The manager then proceeded to walk the guy right outside, grabbed him by the back of his shirt and trousers, and tossed him out the back off of the semi truck dock, just like the bouncers do at the nightclubs. Then he said, "Get out and stay out!" The guy landed flat as a pancake right on top of his big portable stereo and smashed it to bits. After closing and locking the door, we went back up front to take care of the paying customers, and there he was at the front door in his half drunken state, having run around the building to the front. He was waiving to us to come outside and duke it out with him rolling his fists like the boxers of yesteryear. At that moment, a police cruiser pulls right up to the door just in behind him. He turned quite startled, and then took off running. A lady cop jumped out of the cruiser and tackled him into the bushes lassoing him up like in a rodeo or something. She dumped him in the back of the police car, and after getting our story, busted him for armed theft, because he was carrying a switchblade in a leather holster on his belt. That was the last we saw of him. Sorry Charlie, it's just not your day.

"Yep, if it wasn't for theft, all of our groceries would cost 10 cents". This is what I tell many of our customers. Really, it's not far from the truth. The cost of theft puts many small stores out of business. Many of the thieving acts happen right inside the store. Besides grazers, you see all sorts of mind boggling things.

These days, you really have to be prepared for anything. A customer came walking into the front and told us that one of our employees was passed out on the ground outside. After going out front, it was determined that he was knocked out and needed medical attention. The story goes like this:

This particular employee was a younger guy, and he had gone outside to sit and have a smoke. Meanwhile, some big local dude walked up to him and asked him for a cigarette. The employee told him that he didn't have another one, just the one he was smoking. So, the guy told him to give him the one he was smoking. The employee looked at him with a strange look and said, "Are you kidding?" Then, the guy said to him, "Have you ever been knocked out?" Then POW! The big moron punched the employee knocking him out and breaking his jaw with one punch! That was nasty. The employee had to have his jaw wired shut and eat through a straw for some time. You just don't know what kind of crazies you will run into these days.

In times past, the employees were rougher and tougher than the customers. I remember that there was a word that we would use, which meant, all male employees get up front quick, there's a problem. It was quite impressive. Once, there was a male customer causing difficulty, so the manager made the call. Suddenly, all of us guys were arriving up front. The most intimidating were the old butchers. They were big tough guys, used to handling sides of beef, and when they came marching up front wearing their bloody white coats complete with carving knives in their hands and in their hip holsters, they would then ask, "Is there a problem?" That always quieted any scenario very quickly, and the meat cutters always enjoyed getting out of the back for a couple minutes to intimidate troublemakers with their chain mail and bloody knives.

Occasionally, we are confronted with irate individuals who are pumped up with a bit of narcotic juice. One of the plain-clothed security that we had monitoring the store summoned a few of us managers, and told us that he may need some help with a certain guy. This offender had a long ponytail and no shirt, and was pretty big and buff. So, we waited for the cue from the security guard, and when the dude didn't take well to being arrested, then we all ran outside and jumped him in the parking lot. Despite three of us all over him, he kept flailing around, wailing out loud, and trying to get up and run. He was strung out on something. The security guard had a choke hold around his neck. I had one leg pulled back as far as I could. Then, the other manager, pulled back his other leg and then grabbed hold of his pony tail and yanked his head back! We pretty much had to hog tie him to keep him from getting away. He had a little road rash after that. So, if you are going to try to steal from us and run, you should probably wear a shirt.

Another wasted individual that we caught, was hauled back to the office to fill out arrest paperwork. The guy kept yelling and screaming and making all sorts of noise, and although he was handcuffed to a chair, he kept trying to get up and take off running. Two of us had to stand at the door to keep him from trying to bolt. All the while he kept screaming and cussing. Finally, when the authorities arrived, the guy saw that he was going to be taken away, and started directing his screaming at the cop. The cop calmly walked up to the door and told us all to step out for a moment. The door swung shut, and then we heard a good "thwack"! It was the same wonderful sound you hear from a wooden baseball bat, when a player hits a home run.

A couple seconds after the door closed, it swung open again, and the guy was now quietly sitting handcuffed to the chair, but with the dumbfounded look that only a good thump from a nightstick can give you.

These are drastic situations, but you do have to be ready for any of the unusual behavior that people exhibit. It can get ugly. Most behavior is not so violent, it's usually just strange or gross. When I'm working on the floor and filling the shelves, I almost always wear gloves. They help for general purposes, but at the same time, you never know what you're going to stick your hands into. The most common is the trail of peanut shells left all about. You can always find a handful of shells that somebody left behind, as they munch while they are shopping. When in season, there is always a gooey peach pit hidden amidst our displays deposited there by the pit spitters.

Sometimes, you simply have to follow your nose. Walking down the diaper aisle, I noticed that fine scent of a fully loaded diaper, and carefully sifting my way around, I found the deposited diaper that someone left hidden on the shelf, and of course, the torn open diaper package right next to it. Yes, you might notice that there are, on a regular basis, opened diaper bags, where someone has popped one open, took one out, and changed their baby right there on the spot! Despite the offense, I am almost thankful that most persons have the decency to take their dirty diaper with them.

Then again, while following my nose one day, I could

smell a foul scent on the soup aisle. I was trying hard to track it down. Sometimes if a can has been punctured, it smells pretty ornery. Then alas, I found the deceased. I moved a few cans of soup and there it was, a family pack of porterhouse steaks, $25 dollars worth! Somebody decided that they weren't going to buy them, so they put them on the shelf on the soup aisle, and then covered the evidence by placing the soup cans neatly in front of it! It must have been there a couple days, because it was discolored, dripping and stinky. It would have been better if they just threw it on the floor so we could find it and take it to the back, I thought to myself. People are weird.

It happens all day everyday. The items that people don't want, they just throw all over the store, sometimes while you are standing there watching. Right there in the checkstand, while I am looking at them, they shove a discarded item right into the M&Ms or the magazine rack! "If you don't want the item, please give it to me", I say. But the worst is the people who change their mind about purchasing perishable items.

We find them scattered all around. Meat, frozen foods, chicken, shrimp, milk, yogurt, crab, seafood, deli meat, you name it, we find it all over. Besides the fact that we have to throw these items away and take the loss, I just can't believe how many people will wait in line at the deli, seafood, and meat counters, order up very expensive items, have them wrapped up, and then somewhere in the store, change their minds and toss them upon the shelf. It's crazy!

Well, back to the checkstand we go. This changing of the minds leads me to another female phenomena, the pseudo shopper. Many women like picking up items, carting them around the store with them, bringing them up to the check-stand, and then deciding whether or not they will buy them. Normally, to help move things along, people will simply put the items they want to buy right onto the counter and away we go. But for these particular ones, I wait for them to place each item one by one on the counter. They pick up each item, stare at it, calculate the expense, wonder if they really need it, think of the recipe they are making, then place it on the counter. This goes on one item at a time until the basket is empty. Then she hands me the secondary pile and says, "I'm not going to take any of these." In my mind, of course, I ask, "Why did you pick these up, cart them around the store, then decide if you wanted them and make us put them all away? Why don't you just decide before you get up front and make us all wait?" I think it is a security issue, like those who carry half of their belongings with them in their purse. Just knowing it is near, just in case, makes them feel better.

O.k., I have to throw this one out there. Everybody......
Put your home or cell phone number in your wallet or

purse!! You have no idea how many wallets and purses are left at the store, that have every bit of information about your life except the number that we can call to tell you we have your stuff! I remember having to sift through a purse one time, that had, her Id's, credit cards, social security cards, bills, pictures, pink slip for her car, everything. She had her entire life in her purse, except her home phone number! I finally had to call one of her credit cards, to tell them we had her purse, and if they could call her and let her know. It worked, but it would be so much easier if the obvious contact information were there. That includes cell phones, by the way. All we need is a number in your contacts on your cell phone that says, "home".

Most of these things are just common sense, but as you may have noticed, "cents" don't count for much anymore, only dollars, the exception being Coinstar. We have that machine that counts your change for you, for a fee.

I understand the people, who have twenty or thirty dollars or more in change, but now, most kids and young adults will pay 10% and put two or three dollars in change into the machine, then bring the slip up to the checkstand to buy an energy drink. Why didn't they just pay for the drink with their change? You've got me! I don't know. Maybe it gives them that video game high, or it might simply be that all of the lead poisoning from the toys and such over the years has dulled everyone's senses after all.

So, here is a story of common senselessness. Here we were, going about business as usual, and then along comes the neighborhood watchdogs. Well, let me give you a little backround to explain this one. When this particular shopping complex was built, which in addition to our store, contains about two dozen large and small businesses and restaurants, it became quite a large center. When construction began, there were some homes in the neighborhood that were worried about the traffic, noise, and that sort of thing. But because they are up on a hill above the whole complex, the completed shopping center really didn't bother them much. Meanwhile, my friend lives about a half mile up the hill behind the store, and so many times I would stop and see him on my way to work. One day, I saw that construction began on about a dozen new homes on a vacant piece of property directly behind our store and at the same height as the store, not up the hill. I would joke to my friend, and say, "Look, homes for the deaf!" I mean, who in their right mind would pay money to move in behind a grocery store? This all happened at about the beginning of the latest housing boom.

As a side story, not related to the store, but useful in principal, my father, who lives in San Francisco, went looking around for a larger and cheaper place to rent than the place that he had. So, one day, he was looking at a nice apartment.

It was roomy and in good shape. The price was fairly low, so he kept saying to himself, that there must be something wrong with the place. It must be built on burial ground, or the foundation must be cracking, or something, but he couldn't find anything wrong with the place. Then while he was standing there, the place started shaking and rumbling, and finally the great woooooosh and piercing whine of well tuned jet engines at full thrust rushed on by! He then realized that the wonderful apartment he was looking at was right near the end of the runway for the airport! So, he walked out and said, "Forget it, I'll stay where I am at!"

Noting that story, let's return to the store. Now all of the stores in the shopping center, including ours, had been operating for about five or six years before the completion of these homes. Of course, a tall brick wall was built to shield the homes from the complex, but let me give you more of a picture. If you open up the back doors to the receiving area and the semi-truck docks, there is the alley. All large and small trucks delivering to all the stores in the complex use this alley, therefore it is quite busy. The alley is about the width of a two lane street, enough for two trucks to pass each other. Then there is an eight foot brick wall and the new two story houses that reside about ten to twelve feet just beyond that wall. They were built very close to maximize space, but their obvious proximity to the shopping center should tip off anyone considering a purchase of one of these homes.

So, the day arrived, when a group of about six adults and one teenager come up to the front counter and begin to voice their concerns of the neighborhood. For a moment, it was a pleasant break from continually pointing out our return policies to complaining customers. As the one woman of the bunch addressed me, it was obvious that she was the leader and instigator of the group. The others kind of stood back with their arms folded with the look on their face that said, "She made us come here with her...." Turning my attention to her, she then let me have it! She explained that they had all just moved in and that we, the store, were just making too much noise, and that we would have to stop it! She proceeded to explain all the rules that applied about curfews for diesel truck deliveries and decibel noise levels and all sorts of other rules and regulations, almost to the point, that we would simply have to shut down the business. She went on, ranting and raving, the others not saying a word. She wanted to know, who was the boss, who was the owner of the company, who was the property manager, etc. She said she was also going to complain to the city.

I have to say, that I was patient and pleasant, listening to her voice herself, but not having any sympathy or understanding for her at all! I was at complete peace, knowing full well that she had moved in behind a supermarket that had been in operation for years! The market did not move in behind her. That would be a valid reason for a complaint. In addition, maybe she didn't notice that her house cost a couple hundred thousand dollars less than the other houses in the neighborhood for just that reason. After she was finished, I explained to her that there is nothing that I could do, and that she was voicing herself to the wrong person. So, off they went.

Meanwhile, standing there the whole time, the teenage girl remained at the counter. I asked her, "Aren't you with them?" She said, "No", that she was just trying to redeem a lottery ticket. Then she looked left and then right, then leaned over to me and asked, "Are they for real?! Do people really have nothing better to do with their lives, than to complain about the grocery store?" I couldn't believe it. She got it. All these silly adults with their bad decisions and petty grievances just making life miserable for everyone, but this young, 18 year old girl had more understanding than them all! She redeemed my belief in humankind and the younger generation.

This, of course, is not the end of the story. This same woman, whose house was directly behind the receiving door of our store, kept being a constant nuisance for the next couple years. She would climb up on top of the wall and yell at us, when the trucks came. She would take pictures of us and the truck drivers shouting, that she was going to call the police. "Fine, call the police", we would say in return, "We are just doing our jobs." The police would arrive later and ask what was going on. But, by this time, the truck had long since gone. This became so common, that the police would sometimes not even bother coming, because they already knew, that it was simply this lady whining and complaining about the store.

Here's the kicker. Finally after all this complaining to the store, the president of the chain, the property managers, the police, the city councils, and who knows who else, she finally got her way. She got bars and gates installed, with 24 hour guards, so that the trucks can only come in and out during specified times, and the noise had to be kept down as best as possible, meaning that we can't even empty our trash except between certain hours. She was so proud of herself for standing up to all these businesses to improve the quality of her neighborhood and make everyone else's jobs and lives more difficult. Then she sold the place and moved! ....Classic.

Back at my old store years ago, we had other back door problems with the residences across the street. At this particular place, there was a street behind the store. The businesses had about 40 or 50 feet of space to park the trucks to the dock, there was the street, and then apartment complexes, and homes on the other side of the street. When a semi-truck would back into the dock, part of the truck would stick out into the street.

For some reason, the city would not paint the curb behind our store to be used for loading only, so sometimes there would be cars parked that the truck would have to maneuver around. We often thought that we should just paint the curb ourselves, because occasionally, there was bingo night at a church on the corner, and the street would be filled with parked cars. We would then have to go over to the church and ask that they announce that certain cars need to be moved so that our truck may back in.

At the same time, there would be certain tenants in the apartments that did not like the noise of the diesel trucks, despite their cheap rent. They would purposely park their cars right in front of our dock, so that the truck could not back in. Understandable, if there were no more parking spaces left, but the rest of the entire street on both sides would be empty, and it was easy to tell that someone parked just in a certain way simply to be an annoyance. Well, we had to get our work done, so we would do what was necessary. We went out to the parked car and noticed that it was unlocked, so we put it in neutral and rolled it down the street and parked it out of the way, then unloaded our truck. That didn't seem to be much of a deterrent, because a few days later, the same car was parked right in front of our dock again in the same manner, blocking the way for the truck to back in. This time, however, he had locked his car. Realizing that we were well equipped to handle such a situation, we took two of our pallet jacks and a couple of wooden pallets. We put one jack under the front of his car and one under the rear of his car. We then jacked up his car and rolled it down the street, a little bit further than the first time. I think he finally got the point, because after that, he stopped parking in front of our dock.

Moving cars was something we had to do often enough at this particular store and not just from the ones behind the store, but ones right out front too. This was a small older store that was right next to the freeway. So, many times, people with car trouble would pull into the parking lot and then dump their broken car there. It is a very small parking lot, and the people always seemed to abandon their ugly cars right in front, in the best parking spots next to the door. After a couple months, we would realize that nobody was returning for the car. It hasn't been touched and the dust and leaves were accumulating all over it. We would call the city, and they would say that they cannot take it away, because it's on private property. We call up the property owner, and he says he can't do anything about it. Now, after another month or so, we are becoming a bit perturbed about the abandoned vehicle, so we came up with a bright idea.

It was unlocked, so we put it in neutral, pushed it out

back behind the store, and parked it in the middle of the street in the center of the cul-de-sac. It was a dead end street and not in the way of traffic or residences. Needless to say, by the next day, it was gone! It had been towed away. Our plan worked. This became a common thing at this store, having to help abandoned vehicles move along in the recycling chain.

Most people have cars that suit them just fine, and you can tell more about them by seeing what kind of car they have and the condition that it's in. Since we offer help out to the car for anyone who wishes, this only adds to the spice of each day. I'm not sure why, but some of the largest people, drive the tiniest cars, and vice versa. I see some of these 90 pound women climb in behind the wheel of a giant SUV or a monster truck, and they can barely see through the windshield! Then they have piles of groceries and screaming kids. It just makes me want to duck for cover.

Many are very optimistic that they can just come in and get the one or two items that they came in for, not realizing that we are professionals, and we have our store arranged so that you cannot help but buy more than what you need. We will be cooking up sausages or fried chicken, fresh bread from the bakery, and other fine smelling items that gets 'em every time. Then we have great sale items here and there, so that you just can't pass up such a deal. Finally, the candy rack is just sweetening the deal as you wait for the line to move along. That being said, most people end up buying more than they thought. "I only came in for a couple of things", they all say. "That's what we like to hear". Consequently, certain people need a helping hand.

"Would you like help out with that?" Some people end up with two baskets or more, and some with disabilities could always use assistance. Others though, are just tired from the day, and just need a moment of pampering. The one that makes me chuckle, is our super savers. Originally, the "big box" stores began catering to large families, so they could buy a bottle of ketchup the size of a wine barrel for a cheap deal!

Meanwhile, stores like ours started carrying larger size packages of basic items too, and many people enjoy the savings. Now, however, to cash in on those savings, and to stretch their dollar as far as possible, many elderly ones are purchasing these plus size items. Little old ladies come up to the front with a giant tub of cat litter, full cases of bottled water, or a box of laundry soap that will last until kingdom come.

They occasionally haul that moonshine size jug of Burgundy up to the counter, and so I wonder how, after lugging this home, are they going to be able to pour it into a wine glass without drowning themselves in the vat? Maybe they use some sort of pumper to siphon it out. At the same time, their husbands, are herniating themselves and popping disks in their back to lift that 36 pack of beer! They try to lift these things onto the counter, but I just tell them to leave it in the cart, we'll get it. "Why are you buying such large packages", I ask? Maybe they have visiting family. "It's a great deal", they reply, not realizing the possible medical expenses incurred. We then help them out to their car, but I worry about how they are going to haul these things into their house, when they get home.

Just yesterday, an elderly couple comes through, and as I am packing their groceries, the man barks at me saying, "The bags are too heavy! We have arthritis and can't lift anything. Just put one quart of milk in each bag, and make the other ones light!" Strangely, I seem to have noticed that the people asking for us to make their bags light are always buying the heaviest stuff. So, as I am re-packing their goods, his eyes are scrutinizing my every move. Fair enough, I don't mind, but I have to put something in the bags. The "Bag Nazi's", my bosses standing there calculating the cost of each bag I use, and all the "Green" Earth Day movement groan every time we use an extra bag these days. So then, as I completed this particular order and hand him his receipt, he grabs the four remaining bags from the counter with one hand, and lifts them up over the top of the ATM pad and coin machine and down into his cart! Arthritis my foot! I'll give you arthritis! Let me get "Buster" to help you out with that.

"Yes ma'am, we'll take that out to your car for you." Most men don't get help out, even if they need it. They act tough. Many of them have pickup trucks, so they just throw everything in the back anyways. When assisting some others, we get to the door, and then they say, "Oops, I forgot that I drove the sports car today!" So, you try to stuff a full cart of groceries, along with their cases of bottled water and sodas, into every inch of their coupe. "Will you be o.k. driving like that? Can you see out the window?" "Sure, I'm fine", and off they go.

Do you remember when Coca Cola used to come in a big glass bottle? That was the good stuff. Well, we used to have sales on the six packs of the old glass bottles. They were delivered in wooden tray flats. It was classic Coca Cola. Very tasty!

When it was on sale, people would sometimes buy a basket full in addition to their groceries. One older couple did just that, and I then proceeded to help them outside with their stuff. They were driving one of those "Charlie's Angels" style Mustangs from the 70's. So, I packed up their trunk and back seat to the top and still had half a basket to go! Now what? They then told me that they would get into the car, and then I could put the rest of their groceries on top of them. Okay…. So, I packed them in good.

They looked like those people, stuffed into a station

wagon, moving cross country, with only a small portion of the front window to see out of. They smiled and thanked me, and away they went dragging their muffler as they left the parking lot!

Some people, on the other hand, just feel that they don't need our help. Every time I sell a cake, I recall a certain incident that occurred. In our bakery, we will write whatever you want upon the cakes that are already made, or you can custom order a cake of your choice with one days notice. So, one family came in to pick up their large and expensive custom order cake. This thing was about 36" X 24" with writing and decorations all over it. We carefully placed it upon a cart and after they purchased other items, asked them if they would like help out to the car with their cake? "No, we've got it", they reply.

A few moments later, they come back in fully distraught, asking what are we going to do? Now what? Well, as you know, as you exit a store, there is a slight decline going from the sidewalk down into the parking lot. So, as they were exiting, a car was driving past, so they stopped their cart suddenly, and off slid the cake right onto the asphalt! Homemade upside down cake! "We need another cake right away, we are on our way to the party." All of us are just biting our lips, recollecting mentally. We asked you if you wanted help out!! But, nooo, you don't need our help.....Duh!! I take it, that after refusing our help, you want the store to pay for the splattered cake, yes?!" Of course, they do…. Meanwhile, after mentally unrolling my eyes, I have to collect myself to minimize the damage. "We need another cake just like this one!" "Well, sorry, the cake decorator comes in at 2 or 3 in the morning and spends hours working on the custom cakes. She has gone home already, and we are not able to make another cake like the one you dropped. The best we could do is to give you one of our basic decorated cakes that we sell in the display case and write something on it." They didn't care much for that, but they took it anyway, leaving disgusted. Yes, it was all our fault, again.

Yeah, that store was good in some ways, but a pain in others. It was in a nice expensive neighborhood, so people expected to get whatever they want, or else they will send their lawyers in after us. The good part was that they would actually spend money in the store. There is nothing worse than a big complainer, who after all is said and done, is only buying a couple 99 cent items on ad.

There was one store, where I worked for a couple weeks, that was the ultimate grocery store. It was sort of a division of a larger chain that catered to upscale neighborhoods. It had a carport underneath. Then, you would take the elevator up to the store. The entire store was carpeted, so that when you pushed your cart up the aisle, all you would hear is the sound of silence. That place was great, because the people were so rich, that they had no need to complain. Everything was tremendously overpriced and nobody cared. Everything in produce was $4 a pound, although they did have many unique items you don't normally see. I would giggle to myself when I rang up their items, because I generally know what the regular prices are for most things.

Here at this store, they had their own charge card, and this was back before the chains were taking debit and credit cards. I was told never to ask for I.D. for any check written. Just take it. So, the customers would come through, and I would tell them the total. They would just say to me, "Charge it". "O.k.", I said. "Do you have your charge card?" "Nope". "Do you know your number?" "Nope". "O.k., what's your name?" They would just give me their name, and I would look it up on an old green and white computer printout sheet that we had, with a list of all the charge account customers, and then charge it to their account. Then off they went. No card, no I.D., nothing! It just didn't matter there.

The funny part was when their kids would come in. I mean, talk about silver spoons. The kids would wander in after school and grab some snacks. They would come up front and say, "Put it on my mom's account". "O.k., who is your mom?" They would give me a name, and I would put it on the account, and off they would go! Boy, it must be nice.

Meanwhile, with winter arriving and the holidays coming soon, we start to dig in. We pile our backroom full of every sort of holiday food and baking item imaginable and prepare for the onslaught.

One Thanksgiving day, the boss gets a call from a customer saying, "Something is wrong with my turkey! I put it in the oven and it smells bad, and I have everyone coming over tonight!" That manager that I had mentioned before said, "Scott, go save her turkey dinner. Drive this fresh turkey to her house and pick up the bad one." "No problem boss", and so off I went. I delivered the fresh turkey to a happy mom, and picked up the bad bird and brought it back to the store, not realizing the consequences of my stupidity. The woman had wrapped the partially cooked, bad, stinky turkey in a couple plastic grocery bags. Of course, the nasty juice leaked out of the bags all over the carpet in my car! My car stank like bad bird! On top of that, it kept raining for a week straight, so I couldn't even air out my car! I thought I was going to die of the smell. It took months of cleaning and air fresheners to finally rid my car of that nasty scent. Since then, anyone who calls and says they have stinky meat or fermented produce or anything else, I tell them, "Yes, I believe you, throw it away, and just bring the receipt!"

In the old days, we used to be more helpful. The boss used to occasionally let me drive some of the little old ladies home from the store, because they only lived a couple blocks away. The taxi cabs would make them wait for an hour or two, if they came at all, because they hate coming all the way over, only to drive for a couple of blocks for such a small fare.

Many people too, lock their keys in the car or leave their lights on and run down their battery. We used to have a "Slim Jim" and a set of battery cables in the store, and we would regularly break into people's cars to get their keys, or "jump" their car to get it started. Now, with all the insurance issues and lack of general knowledge, we just can't be as helpful as we used to be. That's good and bad I guess. On occasion, some people were a little worried about how quickly we were able to open their car. Now, it's back to every man for himself. These days, even if you help somebody, they tend to scrutinize the manner in which you help. Don't do it like that. Hurry up and get my keys out of the car, I've got places to go. So, my thought bubbles start popping up. "Do you have triple A? No? Maybe you should. . . .

A common problem that grocery stores have is that many people feel free to take the grocery carts home. There are local transients who have a cart that carries what's left of their life to and fro, but there are people, who either have no car or live nearby and simply find it easier to roll their groceries home than carry them.

They then dump the cart somewhere in the neighborhood, where it is absconded and dismantled or used in the next episode of Jackass. Nobody ever takes home the one with the wiggly wheel. Nooo, they always take the brand new shiny carts with the good wheels, and then pulverize them! I've seen carts in the bushes, carts in the river, carts used as planters, etc.... It all stems from the same mentality as those, who throw things about the store that they decide they don't want, and the people who try to return everything but the kitchen sink. They treat the store as if it's their home and everything is theirs to do with as they wish, not realizing that it raises the bill for everyone the next time you shop.

The good metal shopping baskets cost upwards of $500 apiece, so every time the store has to order more to keep a decent supply of carts in the store, it costs quite a bit. It has become quite a business for some, who retrieve the carts scattered throughout town and return them to the stores, for a fee, of course. Even they can't be trusted. At one time, we had to make sure all the carts were inside the store at night, because sometimes, the cart retrieval guys would get the big idea to come and grab any carts that were left outside the store at night in the parking lot, take them away, then return them to us the next day, and bill us for them! There are so many crooks out there trying to make the easy buck, we're lucky to make it home with our pants on. Disappearing carts not only ruffle the feathers of the store owners, but also the store managers, because the cost to replace these carts adds to the store's expenses, which lowers the bonuses the bosses get. So, it becomes the interest of the store manager to keep from losing these carts. That being the case, the managers can get riled up when they see their carts skipping town.

The boss would always tell us to make sure nobody left the parking lot with a cart, but that's easier said than done. Occasionally, we would see him charge out the door and run out to the end of the parking lot and catch someone, who was leaving the parking lot with a cart. He would give them an earful as he would take their groceries out of the cart, set them on the sidewalk, and march back to the store with the basket. The customer would just stand there dumbfounded, not because their groceries were now on the ground, but that someone was running off with their cart! People become very attached to their basket during their short trip in the store. Some really take time to pick out one that they like, so they feel entitled to it, once they get behind the wheel and grip the handle bar. If you bump or move their basket while they are shopping, you get a look like you just scratched their car. I'm going to report you! I hope you have insurance!

We saw the boss come wandering into the parking lot pushing a couple carts one day, so we asked him what he was doing? He said, that on his way to work, he saw a customer pushing her groceries home with our basket about four blocks away. So he pulled his car over, took the basket away from the woman, and pushed it back to the store finding another abandoned basket along the way. It's an epidemic, from the store's point of view.

We once had a system, where by, each customer that would bring a basket out of the store had 25 cents added to their order. Then when they were finished loading their car, they would return the basket to a cart corral, which would spit out a quarter in return. However, the plan didn't work the way the bosses intended. They figured out that the cart nabbers didn't mind paying the extra quarter to wander off with the cart. In fact, they felt as if paying the 25 cents made the cart theirs to do with it whatever they wish. A benefit of this plan was that children all over the neighborhood started collecting the carts and bringing them back to the store to collect the quarters. But eventually, many kids started hanging around the parking lot and begging the customers to let them help with their groceries, so that they could return the cart for their 25 cent tip. Some would try to sneak carts directly out of the store to take them to the return corral to make an easy profit. It wasn't the worst idea, but essentially, the clamor for the loose change became overwhelming, and most people didn't like being billed the extra quarter anyway, so that plan faded away.

Retrieving carts is never the most favored job in the store, although it is good exercise. The carts end up being the last trash dump for people cleaning their cars before they leave the parking lot. All sorts of papers, cans, bottles, fast food remnants, etc. are left behind for us to clean up. Like I said before, "It is a love it or leave it kind of place.", and some employees simply say, "Enough"! I sent out one guy, who had worked at the store for awhile, outside to get carts. He walked out the door, and I saw him wandering back and forth through the parking lot all the way to the end of the complex. He then just kept walking on up the street and kept on going off into the sunset out of sight! We never saw him again! He didn't even come back for his final paycheck. Maybe he was abducted or something, I don't know. He just disappeared. I hope he's doing alright. Few employees quit the store cordially. Usually the last straw is pulled, and out they go in a sudden burst of frustration. It's that family atmosphere that really winds up the tension, and then snap!

The greatest threat to any employee is when they get the word that it's their turn to clean the bathrooms. Preparing them for cleaning a public bathroom is like gearing up for chemical warfare! They put on the virtual gas mask, and heavy gloves, armed with a rapid-fire trigger of disinfectant ammo. They pack up rolls of paper towel as shields to smother the flak and buckshot left behind by the bombardiers, and they are given orders to secure the area!

It's the same as any other public restroom you have ever been in. We try our best to keep it clean and tidy, and people are always glad to know that it is there, just in case. But, the combination of bad hygiene, vandals, internal combustions, sanitary napkins, and various other biohazards really test the employee's resolve and the benefit of their paycheck. As they work, you can see them weighing it in their mind and calculating if it is worth it.

We have tried locking the doors to monitor the entrants, but that becomes a waste of time, and creates other possible problems, because when you have to "go", you have to go! At one store, the restrooms were in the back near the janitor's room. So, when certain customers would find, that the bathrooms were locked and no employee nearby to open them, any room with a pool of water will suffice. On occasion, the mop bucket filled with water to mop the floors would have added surprises from those on the "go"! Needless to say, the locks soon came off the restroom doors.

Yep, that mop sure gets some dirty work. Every now and then, you pick up the scent and spot the trail of a blown daddy diaper. Unfortunately, some elderly and others need to wear the adult diapers that are available for the "loosy goosy", but there are those poor souls that have exceeded capacity. Therefore a trail then begins to form along the floor of the store leading us to the dribbling dumpster, who we then assist to the proper depository. I never forget what one elderly woman said to me, who was a regular shopper for years. She said in the most humble way, "It is terrible to lose control over something you have had control over for most of you life!" I remember what she said, because it would seem to be true for many areas of life. She was a nice lady. Anyway, as you can see, we've got your back....side! O.k., enough potty jokes.

Being that we have so many different kinds of people in every sort of state, you've got to be mentally prepared. We get everything from the humble to the boisterous. We get the loud and the timid. We have the fashionable and the frumpy. Each one has a different personality and mood that you have to adjust to. Most just need a listening ear, but some are on the prowl. That being the case, and the fact that we sell certain aphrodisiacs and all sorts of various shaped produce items, we tend to receive our share of flirting and sexual innuendo. We are professionals, and we are ready for anything, most of which we have heard before.

One of the girls, who was single, finally got sick of the repeated offers for dates, so she bought herself a diamond ring and wore it like a wedding band to ward off advances. It didn't work. Guys still asked her out, and then she would act the part and say, "How dare you ask out a married woman!" I think they could see right through the ring, however. The cheeky expression of a single girl is different from the glow of a married one.

Being in the environment that we are, and the fact that most employees are fairly pleasant, we do have to field our share of advances. Most customers feel comfortable with the employees they see day to day, and so eventually, we get asked out for a date. In our position, you can't just decline and walk away. We have become pretty good at thanking them for their offer, but then still making them feel comfortable enough to keep returning to our place of business. That's talent. But, every now and then, one of the employees will take the offer for a date. Being that we are all like family, word gets around pretty quick. Oh, you are going out with that guy, or that girl? Then everyone who is familiar with that person puts in his two cents. So, for those of you, who want to give it a go, just remember, that if your date goes badly, word of your reputation will be hanging throughout the store.

There was a day, when one of the cute girls who worked in the seafood department came into work with a long face. I knew that she had a hot date the evening before, so I asked her how it went. She said it went well until the middle of the date, while they were out to eat. Although he already knew where she worked, he made the comment that she smelled a little like fish! What a wonderful thing to tell a girl, right? That really makes the date go well. She proceeded to tell me that she knows that she smells like fish, being that she works in the seafood department all day, but for the hot date, she took four showers and scrubbed herself silly.

"I can't smell it anymore, but I know that I smell like fish! I thought that if I scrubbed enough, I could get the fishy smell off of me, but I guess it's probably soaked into me and my clothes." Oh well. She took it in stride and returned to her bubbly self.

Meanwhile, I have had my share of offers while at work. One day, the assistant manager and I were working in the freezer section. A guy came up and asked me where something was located. I recognized him. He was a regular and had come through my line a few times before. Anyway, after asking me the first question, he then proceeded to tell me that he thought that I was nice and wanted to know if I wanted to go out somewhere later. Well, uhphhff, uhh, ummmph, sorry, I'm doing my hair later! I was thrown aback. It caught me completely off guard. I was being asked out by a guy! To put this in perspective, it is like driving down the road and then suddenly putting your car in reverse. Usually, as a guy, I am thinking of ways to meet girls and to think up pick up lines to use. Most girls are thinking about new ways to reject the offers coming their way. So, all of the sudden, I had to switch my mind from the offensive to the defensive. I had to quickly think up all the rejection lines I had ever received and pull one out of the hat! I can't even remember what I replied to him, but he turned and went on his way. I stood there dumbfounded. The assistant manager who was working nearby looks over at me with a strangely curious look, and asked, "What was that?" I looked over at him and said, "Boss, I have just been asked out by a guy!" We both just shivered for a moment, and not because the freezer was cold. It was the 80's, and this sort of thing wasn't as popular as it is today. Needless to say, word got around the store pretty quick, and I got a good share of jeers and whistles that night from my fellow employees. I then realized, that I was perceived as being available on both sides of the fence. It wouldn't be the last time I would have to guard my backside!

In most cases, I am the recipient of the offer by a mother to date her daughter. I am one of those guys that mothers really like. It's a tragedy. No girl wants to date someone her mother likes. I tried a couple of those, but they really didn't work out very well. I guess you learn along the way. Sometimes you think that you are prepared for anything, but inevitably, there is a new surprise.

There was a foreign lady that would come in shopping with her two daughters, and as I would ring up their groceries, she would comment about how cute I was, and that her daughters were available.

The daughters would just look at me and smile with a bashful gleem. Every time they would come shopping, the mother would continue making the offer giving me a few extra incentives, and each time increasing the innuendo. Finally one day, as I was ringing up their groceries, she was explaining to me in her broken English that she has taught her daughters many things. I looked at them and smiled, saying "Great". It was then that she held up a small brown paper bag. She popped open the bag and quickly showed me the sex toys inside! Holy Cow! I was trying to keep my composure, but it was difficult to continue concentrating on my work, and I was turning a bit red at that point. The three girls then began to giggle. Yep, there's not much left to say after that, just a lot of giggling. Intrigued, my mind weighed the possibilities in a flash, but I said to myself, I think I'd better pass on that one.

I was molested once! Well, not exactly. But here's how it went. I was asked to help out at a different store for a couple days, and so I went. I wasn't there ten minutes, before the boss, whom I was speaking with, got a call on the "com" line saying that a certain regular wacky lady had come in. The boss put down the phone and looked at me, and told me that my first job of the day was going to be to take care of "Mary". So, I went downstairs and introduced myself to her and asked her if she needed any help. Now, Mary was an older lady with a few screws loose. Every store has someone similar. She talks out loud to herself and to anyone that walks by, especially young kids. She wants to give them all a hug and a kiss, essentially scaring the daylights out of them with her mustache and nasty teeth. So, for this day, it was my job to keep her occupied and away from other customers until she got her groceries and left. Meanwhile, she would be rubbing my arm and telling me how cute I was, as I tried to help her remember what she came in for. After forty minutes of this, I finally brought her up front and rang up her groceries. She said she wanted to wait inside until her cab came by, but I convinced her that it was a nice day out, and that she should sit outside in the sunshine. So I walked her out, and found her a good spot far away from passing customers. She was still holding my arm, and as I was saying farewell, she reached down and rubbed my family jewels and asked me if I wanted to come over to dinner that night! Somehow, I was able to resist that offer. Finally, I strolled back into the store and noticed all the employees ready to burst out with laughter. I walked up to the front desk and told the boss, " I think I need a shower!" I was then informed that I was now properly "broken in". The rest of the day seemed to go so easily after that.

There are a few employees that don't take the flirting

and advances well, but most are comfortable with themselves and do just fine. In a place, where you see the same people over and over, you've got to expect that people will form an attachment to you. You are a friendly face. But you really have to be prepared for the unexpected. Well, as best as you can be, I guess.

Like I mentioned before, times have changed, and there is a lot of gender bending going on. When I first began work at the store, the men wore aprons, and the women wore smocks, which were essentially a zip up pull over. So, it was easy to tell what's what. Eventually, they got rid of the smocks and we all wore aprons. At one point, there was a shift to polo shirts, but now, we are back to aprons, and there was still this side of the fence or that side, seeing that men would wear ties, and women would wear a frilly bow tie looking thing. But as the 90's came to a close, the fence was being torn down and the bending was becoming more pronounced.

Essentially, a couple of the girls started wearing the men's ties. One wore it, because she had a large neck, and the woman's tie would not fit, and the other said that the men's tie was more comfortable. So, time goes on, and I was transferred to a different store, and low and behold, all of the women were wearing men's ties. I made light of the behavior, but was rebuffed with inquiries of the era I come from.

Had my day passed already? Well, I became content with the new age and still felt that I could fit in, until one day, when a certain employee came in to work. Then I realized that I am far removed from the modern age. I would call him Michael, but he would quickly retort, "No, it is Mik-A-el". As I'm sure you have concluded, Mike is a bit light in the loafers. He would usually come in to work dressed a bit daintily, talk with a lisp and carry his own make-up bag. But this one day, he came in wearing a pink undershirt under his white work shirt (which made his shirt look pink) and he was wearing one of the frilly girl ties! E-Gads! Yep, the world has turned upside down, and I have been left hanging there. Well, things went about as expected. He got yelled at for his choice of dress and later for not finishing his work, and so he cried and quit, then moved on to another job that more suited his style.

As we all continue to find our place in the world and go back to business as usual, most people are fine paying customers, although they may give complaints as to the rising cost of things. All the food growers have been watching the gas companies and saying, hey, we can produce less and charge more too!

It's a shame, because it used to be, that cooking at home would cost about 1/3 or 1/4 of what it would cost to eat out. Now, it's almost even. Unless you are buying in bulk sizes for a large family, it is almost cheaper to eat out, not even considering the cleanup. These days, people are feeling a bit cheated, and so they should. The big chains haul oranges from Florida to California and vice versa, then pass on the costs of shipping to the consumer, when all the while, we already have oranges growing right here in California, just a few miles away. You get the idea. Moaning and groaning are so commonplace now, that I don't even here it anymore. It sounds like a dental office, when I ring up each item. Oooh, aahh, ouch, uuhh, Rrrrr, what? Wait a minute, how much was that? Being that the prices are marked on the shelf, I think the oooing and aaahhhing is just people's way of venting their frustration concerning rising costs.

Now, even if people are good at math, they usually let the numbers float about their brain like lottery balls. Nobody really wants to know the total. They always hope that it will somehow be cheaper than what they imagined. Knowing that, the store slyly plays the numbers game. Instead of marking something $1.00, they mark it 10 for $10.00. People then feel they are getting a better deal by buying ten. Then the store really throws people a curve by marking something 3 for $8.00, or similar odd numbers that really stunt their thinking. Most people's minds turn to flubber by that point as they try to divide 8 into threes, so they just screw it and buy three.

One elderly character came in and bought some groceries including some oranges that were on sale. He asked, "How much did you charge me for those oranges?!" Well, they are on sale, 4 lbs. for $1.00. "What!? I thought that they were 4 for $1.00". "No", I told him. "They are 4 pounds for $1.00." "Take them off then", he demanded. "But they are only 68 cents when I ring them up by the pound. It's cheaper." "Forget it!", he yelled. "I don't want them!" "However you like it." I should have just charged him a dollar and made him happy. I've learned my lesson. If it isn't right in their mind, don't even try to persuade them otherwise. The customer is always right. Right? Cough, cough, Ahem.

Everyone has his own little way to combat the system. You have some people, who think they have been taken advantage of, who become moochers and feel entitled to a free fried chicken leg or other snack while they shop, and you have a few that are just trying to somehow get back at the financial business system.

You have your general thievery. But every now and then you just plain get robbed. Fortunately, most armed robbers stick to the liquor stores and convenience stores, but occasionally, you get one who goes for the big one. There are so many cameras and security devices in stores these days, which help as a deterrent, but sadly, most of them are pointed at the employees. Currently, there are many stores that have banks inside, and the banks are also targets of robbery.

Oddly enough, not that I mind, the supermarkets themselves don't really see too many armed robbers.

I happened to be working, the last time the bank inside our store was robbed at gunpoint. I was outside talking to a customer, and a Chevy Suburban went screeching out of the parking lot. The customer and I looked at each other, and I said, "Boy, they are sure in a hurry to go somewhere!" So, when I walked back into the store, it was quite empty and quiet up front. I walked down the aisles and noticed there were customers in the back of the store peeking up the aisle. So, I walked over to them and ask if they needed any help? They looked at me and asked if it was safe to come out? "Safe to come out?", I asked. She said to me, that they were told to go to the back of the store, because we were being robbed! "Really", I said. So I walked back up to the front of the store, and noticed the store employees up front coming down from their adrenaline rushes, and the bank employees were white as ghosts! "The bank was just robbed", a fellow employee told me. "Wow", was all I could say. Even an indirect brush with a robbery gives you a quick rush. Then I realized that it was the getaway car that I had seen tearing out of the parking lot! So, as the police arrived, I was able to describe the Suburban and eventually rode with them to identify the vehicle that had been abandoned in a shopping center down the road. That was a wild day.

Years ago, there were some bandits that were hitting grocery stores along freeways. They would rob the store, and then jump on the freeway with their car, making them difficult to spot. So, as a precautionary measure, due to our proximity to the freeway, some silent alarm devices were planted in our stores. The way it worked was, there was a little box in each register till. Then two $20 bills were placed between connectors in the box, so that if the bills were removed, the silent alarm would sound. It was a good idea. It did have a drawback, however. A few times it happened, that a clerk would accidentally pull the bills out of the box, and minutes later, the store would be surrounded by cops with their guns drawn!

The boss would have to call in a false alarm and walk outside with his hands up, and let the police know that everything was alright. It was a bit nerve racking to those present, customers and employees, being surrounded with guns pointed your way! Eventually, it was too costly to keep paying the police for false alarms, and they did catch those freeway bandits, so it was back to our usual routine.

I was once a suspect for a robbery! One day, I had just come from the beach and stopped in my store to get a sandwich from the deli. I had parked in front of the bakery shop next door. After going home and sitting down to enjoy my sandwich, I get a call. It was the police! They said, "We have you and your house surrounded. Come out with your hands up to the end of your driveway." I thought that it might be a joke or something, but I did like they asked. I walked down my driveway still wearing my swimming trunks but with my hands up. As I reached the street, the cops came up to me with their guns drawn, and then realizing I was not the person they were looking for, began to ask me some questions. They eventually noted that they were looking for a blonde man, which I am not, and that there was a robbery in the store shopping center. I told them, that I work there, and asked what had happened. It turns out that the bakery next door had been robbed and they saw my car leaving at the same time as the robbery suspect. My car, at the time, couldn't be more conspicuous if I tried! It was a bright blue VW bug with colored stripes on it! Not exactly the best car to have in a getaway.

So, here is the fun part. That afternoon, I was scheduled for work, so I come driving into the parking lot and parked right in front of the bakery. I could see it in their faces inside, "Oh noooooo, He's back!! As I walked into the store to work, all the employees were yelling, "Get down, the robber is here!" ,they having heard about the robbery from a bakery employee, who told them that the robber had got away in a blue VW bug with colored stripes on it. Everyone at the store knew whose car that was. We all got a big kick out of it, despite the robbery itself, although I still think it made the bakery employees nervous every time I pulled up for work.

Working at the store with fellow employees is like being part of a platoon or some other military group. You are thrown together with people of all sorts to battle for the cause, ('cause they're hungry!). It is the same at most jobs, I guess. Going through difficult times and circumstances brings an odd group closer together. We become almost like brothers and sisters.

In many cases, you spend more time with your workmates than you do with your family. Being in such proximity day to day and dealing with all sorts of strange and unusual behavior from the public, it just lays the perfect foundation for a nice practical joke. We could all use a good yuk or two from time to time. Obviously, some jokes can get out of hand or stray into the shady or lewd behavior of the mental midgets, so according to the store, "….horseplay is grounds for termination…." That's the judgment held over our heads. You can be fired for just about anything these days. At some point, however, you have to help ease the tension, and nothing beats a good practical joke.

Things can get a little boring and monotonous standing in the checkstand repeating yourself over and over. I get caught by some customers, every now and then, repeating my lines out of order, so they ask, "Is this a recording?" After snapping out of my funk, I say, "Yes, keep your hands and arms inside the vehicle at all times" Some people say to me, "You probably do this in your sleep." "Not anymore", I reply. When I first began working in the checkstand, I would work all day, then after going home, I would dream all night that I was checking. Then when I would wake up, and have to go to work again thinking, I just got off 16 hours work, 8 hours awake, and 8 hours asleep! I wish I would've been paid for the virtual overtime.

Sometimes in the midst of my rut, a little light comes on, and a silly idea pops into my head. It's time for a practical joke. Occasionally, I find in the till a piece of a $1 bill, or $20 bill, etc. Usually it's a corner piece, the bigger the better. I then take a little piece of tape and grab a magazine from the rack at the checkstand area. I pick an odd one that most people would not normally read, like "Pregnancy" or something. Then I open it up and tape the piece of the bill with the corner sticking up out of the top of the magazine, so that when you put it back on the shelf, it looks like a magazine with real money sticking out of it! Then I wait. It's not long before someone spots the booty. I saw a guy come into my line and load his groceries onto the counter. He then sees the magazine. His eyes look left and then right, and he casually reaches for the magazine and opens it up as if he is interested in the literary content. Upon finding he has been short changed, and that he had been "got", back to the rack went the magazine. I always love that one, it works every time. The best part is, they don't realize that it was me who set the trap, and that I saw the whole thing. It's the little things.

You can only play mini jokes on the customers, so eventually, we start to focus our strategies on each other. Do you remember those large glass bottles of Coca Cola I was telling you about earlier? It was the drink of choice for most everyone at the time, but especially for those on night crew.

When you work graveyard, you tend to drink plenty of soda, and everyone used to drink the large glass bottles of Coke. So, being that there was usually a small group of people working late and there were open bottles of soda around, things were ripe for diabolical tampering. Every now and then, you would finish working an aisle, and then go to grab your soda for a swig, and then surprise....! One of my friends I worked with, took a drink of his soda and then let out a gasp and AAAUUUGGGHHH! Someone had sprinkled a couple of those little packets of pepper into his soda and spiced it up a bit. "I'll get you back", he said, and so it continued. Another fine day rolls around and the practical joker goes to take a drink of his soda and as he pulls it away from his mouth, a slimy string stretches from his lips to the bottle! He had been gotten. Someone had put a raw egg into his bottle of soda making it a bit gooey. "I'll get you...."

Meanwhile, as the opportunity rose again another day, my friend goes to take a drink of his soda. He lifts the bottle high in fine Coke commercial style, and nothing comes out! He pulls it down and sees that the cap is off, so he raises it up again, and nothing comes out. Puzzled, he wiggles it, then looks, and upon closer inspection, realizes that a tampon had been shoved into the bottle and was working spectacularly! EEEWWWwww! And so it went, as the creative additives continued to jostle the already lively nature of night shift.

That same friend had finished up his work one evening, and he was collecting his stuff to go home, but he couldn't find his sweater. So, he looked about and finally, one of his fellow workers hinted that he should look in the freezer. Well, it was there all right. One of his buddies had soaked his sweater in water and then hung it in the freezer. It was frozen solid! Instead of a "pushup", he got a frozen pullover!

At our break table, we have the tray of usual condiments like salt & pepper, sugar packets, and of course the community bottle of hot sauce. Well, it just so happened that the hot sauce ran out, and one of the employees, who was well intentioned, refilled the bottle with his favorite hot sauce. Over the next couple days, I noticed that a number of the other employees on lunch were gasping a bit heavily and their eyes were welling up.

After a few of them expressed their curiosity concerning

the hot sauce, the one employee happily fessed up and told them that the community sauce had run out, and that he had refilled the bottle with his favorite habanero sauce! That's one way to get the employees fired up.

One of the girls at my store, who seems so passively mellow, is the perpetrator of the oldest practical joke of all time, the old jack-in-the-box routine. She will climb into the large trash can and pull the lid over her, so that when the unsuspecting target walks up, Boooo!! She pops out of there making their hair stand up straight! Got 'em again.

Speaking of Boo, Halloween comes around every year, and we always get sent the latest goodies and costumes to set up on display for everyone. They come out with some pretty good rubber masks of various gruesome creatures these days. This one in particular was the abominable snowman. It looked like a vicious sharp toothed gorilla with white straggly hair, perfect to scare someone with….and I knew just the right person. There was a girl, who took over working the liquor department after I had moved on to a different department. There was a little room in the corner of the department that was used for the fire risers and subbed as a little office. Essentially, you had to take a full step into the room in order to turn on the light, so it became a perfect spot for my trap.

It was early in the morning, so I took the ugly ape mask

and strung it up in such a way, that when you opened the door to the liquor room, the mask would swing down right at you toward the door. The trap was set.

About a half hour later, we were not open yet, and I had kind of forgotten about the trap I set. I was up at the front desk sorting some paperwork, and then the store manager comes waddling up front dragging his feet. His jaw was wide open and he had a dumbfounded look on his face, and he said, "Scott, you won't believe it! I just walked into the liquor room to check on the fire risers, and a big white hairy gorilla came swinging down and hit me in the face! It scared the hell out of me!! At least I am wide awake now." "You walked right into my trap! It wasn't meant for you." I told him. "That was a good one", he said as he waddled off to his office.

After that, I quickly went back to the liquor department and set it up again. About ten minutes later, the liquor girl comes running up to the front screaming. She ran right up to me and started beating on me saying, "I know it was you….!"

She looked at me with her bright eyed startled look and said, "I went into the liquor room to get my stuff, and this big white hairy gorilla came swinging down and poofed me in the face! While screaming, I thought, Scott is standing right behind me laughing at me, so I jumped and turned around, and you weren't there! I knew it was you though!"

It was beautiful. I got two people with one trap within ten minutes!

Speaking of ugly heads, we sell many unusual animal parts at the meat counter, and one of the items we sell is labeled "Cabeza de Rez". It is wrapped in so much plastic wrap that you cannot tell what's in there, but if you speak Spanish, you know that it's a cow's head! Well, when these things come in from the warehouse, they are not yet wrapped, and the head is skinned and frozen solid with the tongue hanging out of its mouth. So, we would set it up just inside the freezer door, and then go up front and tell one of the young female baggers to put some ice cream away in the freezer in the back. They would open up the freezer door and would be scared stiff seeing the cow's head staring right at them! They probably thought that the meat cutters had some kind of cult ritual going on back there or something.

While in the back one day, sorting through the carts of go-backs and markdowns, I came across a fuzzy mouse cat toy that was missing the UPC label. The old prankster light came on, and I said to myself, I know just what to do with this one. So, off to the bakery I went.

I took the little mouse and hooked a string about two feet long to it and taped it to the bottom of the freezer door on the inside. It was set up in a way, so that when you opened the freezer door in the work area of the bakery, the string would pull on the little fuzzy mouse and make it seem as if the mouse came running out of the freezer. I came back a short time later to find the cake decorator completely flushed red. I asked her if she had seen my fuzzy mouse running around, and she shouted, "That was you?! I went into the freezer and that thing came running out and scared me to death!" "Perfect", I said. Then she told me that it was a great joke, and that I should set it up again, so we could get somebody else. So I did. I went away and continued with my work, leaving my new accomplice to finish decorating her cakes. A short time later, the decorator told me that as she worked, she watched as the bakery manager open up the freezer door making the mouse run out, and she jumped straight in the air not making a sound! She too, agreed it was a good one, and that it got her heart going! The fun that you can have with string is endless.

One joke that was played was also educational. We had a new bread delivery guy come in the back receiving door to make an order to deliver some name brand bread. Meanwhile, another driver from the same company but a different division also arrived to bring in pastries. He had noticed that the bread driver left his keys in his delivery truck. That's a no-no. So, the pastry driver hopped in the bread truck and parked it around the corner of the building. He then told me the story, and asked me to make sure that the bread driver didn't call the police. Finally, after the bread driver strolled outside to bring in his order, he came running back in. "Someone has stolen my truck!!" After playing dumb and letting him sweat for a moment or two, the pastry driver put his arm around him and walked him out back around the building explaining the lesson he had just learned. I'll bet he never did that again.

Now, here is a practical joke that was never meant to be played. It fell upon a few unlikely customers, but I wish we could have seen it. Once, as we were working in the dairy box, we came across a problem. We try our best to rotate everything around, so that the customer gets the freshest product and we keep the inventory rotated. We regularly spend time checking the code dates on the items in the dairy to ensure freshness. Then we came upon an unusual one. We were checking the code date on a can of Reddi Whip, the spray on whip cream that comes in a can. Usually, the dates on those are months ahead, but on this occasion, we looked, and the cans on the shelf were over six months out of date! Somehow, this one case of product had escaped rotation somewhere along the line. We pulled the remaining cans off the shelf and took them to the trash in the back. We usually open any product thrown into the dumpsters to ensure, that no dumpster divers pull out any bad food from the trash and get sick. So, as we pop the cap on the Reddi Whip and spray, the whip cream must have shot out about 20 feet! The pressure had built up inside the cans over the span of time, which turned the cans into little shot guns of whip cream! It was relatively entertaining, until we realized that we only threw out about seven cans, and that the others in the case had been sold to customers! We could just picture granny asking if you would like a little whip cream on your pie, and then firing a blast of cream all over some little tike. It cracks me up just thinking about it! I keep waiting to see if it ever appears on "Funniest Home Videos".

Other foods can also be a good form of entertainment and a little dangerous too. Do you know those pop n' fresh biscuits, that come in the tube? Well, every now and then, when checking the dates on those items, we come across a few, way in the back, that didn't make it through the rotation. We pull them off the shelf, pop them open and throw them into the garbage. However, being that it is a fermenting type food with yeast in it, it continues to expand all of this time. You may occasionally see popped open packages on the shelf. Some, on the other hand, hold tight until you pop the cork, like a bottle of bubbly. So, as we began to discard these biscuits, we would tap the metal ends of the tubes on the brick wall to pop them open, and then POOF! The biscuits shot out of there like a canon. For some reason, it is quite hilarious to see biscuits fly across the room! A similar thought crossed our mind as we popped open the flying dumplings. We wondered how many people bought some of the canisters, before we pulled them off the shelf? POOF.... dinner on the fly!

Anyway, just to let you know, if you have any leftover dough, it makes perfect ammunition for a biscuit fight. Chucking dough at one another eases tension, and gives just the right amount of sting upon impact. So, if you need a little exercise and want to vent some frustrations with friends or family, pop open a tube of uncooked biscuits for an appetizing food fight.

But, when all is said and done, some of the best all around fun you can have is with a plain old squirt gun. I often have my keychain sized "super soaker" loaded in my apron pocket just in case. It not only is an attention getter, but it's fun to squirt fellow employees when they are not looking, and watch them look around wondering where the rain is coming from. I just put my head down and keep working. They're stupefied.

Working in the daytime is fine, but when you work the evening shift, like I usually do, it tends to be a bit more interesting. If you didn't already know, things definitely become more unusual on a full moon. After observing people for all these years, I've come to the conclusion, that whatever weirdness you have, it becomes most prominent on a full moon. For instance, if you are the hairy type that likes to creep around the neighborhood and bite people, well you would most likely do so on a full moon. Me, I'm a sarcastic joker. So, I tend to be even more so when the moon is bright. You get the idea. Some people become more irritable. They drive with road rage in the parking lot.

They might give me a severe tongue lashing, because they were charged a dime too much for something. By the way, these are the same ones, that won't pick up a dime off the ground if they see it. Then you see some ghouls creeping around the store, some trying to figure out what they would like to steal tonight, and others lurking about, waiting for the opportunity to paint hieroglyphics on the wall in the bathroom. They are so proud to be able to write their name. In what language, I'm really not sure.

One of our baggers came inside after collecting carts in the parking lot. She had a stunned look on her face, and said that some old lady just hit her with her car outside! We weren't quite sure if she was serious, so we asked what happened? She then told us that as she pushed a row of shopping baskets up to the front of the building, there was an old lady, who couldn't wait to leave the parking lot and was mad that she had to wait for the bagger to push the carts out of the way, so she honked her horn making gestures. The bagger continued to push the carts forward and so the lady put the car in gear and bumped the bagger in the legs with her car's bumper! She wasn't hurt at all, but she was stunned that the crabby old lady actually hit her with her car. It was the holiday season, and the parking lot was packed, so she would have only moved forward a car length or two anyways. Maybe she was the ghost of Christmas past and she was late. 'Tis the season....

There are often things that we want to say to correct the behavior of shoppers or their children, and sometimes we do, to our dismay. We've come to the realization that these people don't just have bad habits, they want to be this way. Really then, we just help make people become more irritating, because essentially, they enjoy being irritants. Every now and again, other customers will try to come to the rescue and point out certain unacceptable behaviors. Then here we go again.... It's a fight!

No matter how well meaning someone intends to be, or how politely they convey themselves, I have never seen anyone ever accept the criticism of another shopper. Like I mentioned, this would be like insulting someone in their own home. But at the same time, the one doing the criticizing feels that someone else is misbehaving in their home. So, a fight always ensues. Sometimes it's a verbal barrage and a swordsman match of the tongue. Sometimes it's a New York style insult square off. But many times, it just gets physical.

There was a female customer, who proceeded down the potato chip aisle. She then came upon a group of unruly siblings from about 10 years old down to about 2. We had already tried to reason with the mother concerning her children's behavior, but to no avail. The older kids had decided to walk down the aisle punching all the bags of potato chips along the way. Then of course, the pecking order ensued, so that all of the children are punching the chips, and the three year old is punching and kicking all the bags on the bottom shelf. The other female customer, who was obviously a mother also, began mildly scolding the children concerning their destructive behavior. Flabbergasted, the children's mother comes unglued! How dare you correct my children, who do you think you are, ...filthy filth filth, dirt, flyin', stinkin', mahem, etc.... It was an unusual fight. First you had the proper, well dressed, refined mother. Next you had the raw, sloppy, mud wrestling, trailer trash mother. Each of which had a distinct advantage, but neither really getting the edge on the other. Now that it had become a scene, we had to jump in there and break it up. We pretended like we were listening to both sides of the story, but we already knew the scoop. We had enough of the Neanderthal family, so we threw them out. Unfortunately, it was just another episode of the shopper's family feud.

Children are much more prone to accept adult correction, when their parents are not around to defend their atrocities. One evening, I was facing the store, making everything look full and flush. I had just finished the toilet paper and paper towel aisle. Then after moving on, some children came wandering down the aisle knocking down all the work I had just finished. One of the female employees, who was big and burly, saw what the kids were doing and gave them an ear tugging, big mamma's house earful. She scolded the kids telling them, "Scott just finished working hard to get this aisle looking nice, and here you are knocking it all down again! Now you kids are going to stay here and put it all back up and make it look nice again right this minute!" Afterward, she told me what happened, so I peeked around the corner and sure enough, there were the two kids working hard putting it all back up again. Yes ma'am.

Back at my old store, we had things pretty good. There was an Italian pizza joint in the complex that delivered. Sometimes they would have an extra pizza, and they would bring us a freebee. In the old days, when our deli would close up, they would put all the leftover fried chicken in bags and sell it cheap. By the end of the night, it was mostly wings or drumsticks.

Yep, there's nothing better than cheap food. Even the local bums could eat good on those nights. Every now and then, we would order a pizza from another popular delivery place. After delivering, they would grab a few things from the store, and then they realized that we had cheap chicken late at night. We would eventually get sick of eating chicken, and they would get sick of pizza, and so it was. Every now and then, the guys at the pizza place would call and ask if we wanted to trade a pizza for the fried chicken? Sure, why not. We would buy the cheap chicken and trade it for the pizza! What a deal! That didn't last too long though. Someone in Buffalo came up with this idea of "hot wings", and so the price of chicken wings shot up. No more leftover wings, but we had a good run.

People often excitedly ask if we get a discount for working at the store. "No way", I tell them. "I wouldn't want a discount at the store even if they offered it." I explain that if I got a discount, then I would be shopping day and night. My friends would be bugging me, my mom would be bugging me. Everyone would pester me to do their shopping for them, because I would get a discount. They agree that it is probably for the best.

Here we are, finishing another evening at work. We are wrapping up all the loose ends and getting our minds prepared to go home. Then look. Oh no, here comes the "caboose lady"! We gave her that name, not just because she has a big caboose, but because she would always wear a train engineer's hat. We felt bad for her in a way, because she was missing a screw or two, but at the same time, she was always quite the annoyance. She didn't drive, so she would come walking to the store dragging one of those pull carts, that the old ladies use. We would see her coming down the street on her way to the store, and we would just sigh.

On a usual day, she would come in the line and halt all activity. We would ring up one item at a time, and she would be constantly checking the amount after each item to make sure she had enough money. You get used to her, except for the fact, that she would usually come in ten minutes before we close and then do coupon shopping for a half hour or so after we are already closed, meaning that we couldn't finish our work and go home. When we would see her come down the street late at night, we would shout "Choooo Chooooooo", ding, ding, ding, ding, caboose crossing! Many times, we would try to help her shop for the things she wanted. She didn't care much for that.

Sometimes, we would turn off all the lights in the store except for the one above the checkstand. She would just keep shopping using a flashlight. A couple times, when we would see her coming, we would push the clock ahead a few minutes and lock up the doors, telling her to come back tomorrow, we are closed. That was kind of mean, but sometimes you just don't feel like having to explain the overtime to the boss, and you just want to go home already.

One night, after she had kept us there late on overtime, we finished her order and then locked the door behind her. She would always spend a few minutes rearranging and re-bagging all her groceries outside before leaving. Then, she starts knocking on the door. "I got the wrong tortillas. Can I come in and exchange them?" "No", we reply. "We closed a half hour ago. Come back tomorrow." Then again she asks, "Can I exchange my tortillas?" She wouldn't leave. She then tried to slide the tortillas under the door. She kept knocking, etc. We finally finished our paperwork and so forth, and we opened the door to go home. She was still out there holding her tortillas. You want to feel bad, but there is a difference between being needy and being annoying. She was just an-noying.

After working at a few different stores, you realize, that all the customers are the same, just the faces change. There is a "caboose lady" at every store, someone that slides their foot in the door just before closing and coupon shops, not letting you close the store and finish your work. Then, there are always two transient drunks that come in and smell to high heaven. There is the other annoying lady that doesn't stop talking.....ever! She is a bit off her rocker and rambles on and on to every employee, customer, or person that comes near, talking about God knows what. So no matter where you go, it's always the same.

Each store also has a secret boozer. We regularly find a half empty bottle of hooch somewhere in the store. I don't know whether they just chug it, or pour it into another container, but that one always perturbs me. I'm not so disappointed that they stole the liquor. That happens all the time. I just can't believe that half a bottle gets wasted every time! If you are going to steal it, finish it! What a waste.

Some of the new employees get upset, when we miss catching a thief. I tell them not to worry, they'll be back. You see, people who steal are morons. That is why they steal.

Then, of course, after getting away with it, they say to themselves, that was easy. So, being stupid, they come back and try it again another day. We eventually bust them. They become obvious fairly quickly, because they always try to increase their haul on the next run.

There was one guy that we never caught though. I still wonder who he was. For a long period of time at my old store, almost every night, we would find a half empty bottle of flavored schnapps. It became a game for us at night. O.k., who can find the half empty bottle of schnapps tonight? As we went up and down the aisles cleaning the store, eventually one of us would find it. Sometimes it was peach, sometimes blackberry, etc. We never did catch that guy. Usually we have an idea of who it might be, but this guy was good. He always eluded us. Cheers.

While I am on the subject, I have to let you know that I have solved one of the mysteries in life that we all have wondered. The answer is, Yes. The guys standing at the side of the road with the cardboard sign use your money to by boose. I know that they all have a good story. They are veterans, or homeless, or need gas for their car, and many people feel that they might make good with some of the money. In reality however, they buy alcohol. I have worked at stores in bad areas and good. I worked at one store, where the homes behind the store cost 1.5 million dollars. Guess what? The store still had its fill of regular daily street drunks. I know it seems heartless, but most of these ones are quite capable to wash themselves up and work at our store. If they want to work for food, let them. Many of them are actually a bit intellectual. They just have issues like the rest of us. If you saw them everyday, like I do, you would know that you are doing them a favor by not giving them money. P.S.—Just recently, one of the daily drunks at the store in the rich area I mentioned, came shopping in the store I am currently at. He has gotten off the sauce, got himself a job, and is doing much better now. Way to go buddy!

As a boozer, some come up with a few antics. We were opening up the store one morning and one of our local bums comes crawling down the ladder from our attic. He had snuck up there the previous evening, when nobody was looking, and crashed there all night! He must have been hammered, because he slept soundly enough not to move and set off the store's alarms. You know what the odd thing is. As unsightly and gamey as they look and smell, they are usually better behaved than many of our other customers.

One Brooklyn New York couple that came in were incessantly abrasive with each other. They were hilarious to observe. I thought I was watching a t.v. "sitcom". They were in their late fourties to early fifties, so you knew this was an ongoing theme. They would talk trash to each other using every colorful name in the book. It almost sounded natural when you included the strong accent. All the while, he had one of our ads that he had rolled up and waved around like a scepter. Each time his wife would say something silly (all the time), or when he just wanted her attention, he would whop her with the ad on her arm or even on the top of her head, just like you would wallop your dog with the newspaper, when it misbehaved! Hey baby, (WHOP) what'r ya' buyin' that fer? Stop hittin' me you bastard, I'll get whatevr' I wanna'! They cracked me up. I mean, it was like watching, The Honeymooners, I Love Lucy, All in the Family, Sanford and Son, Married with Children, and The Simpsons, all in one show! Buy the time they finally left the store, he had worn out our advertisement by beating her with it. I felt bad at first, until I realized that they were perfect for each other.

There was another odd couple at the store in the rich area, who would come in every other day and go to our service deli. They would order a couple items, do a little other shopping, then come to the front and ask for the manager. Every time they would come in, they would complain about the service they received from a certain Middle Eastern girl that worked back there. This would happen multiple times a week. Essentially, what it came down to was, that they didn't like the way she looked or spoke, so they wanted her fired. They would complain to me, my boss, and even complain to the corporate office. These people were simply pests, and for some reason, they had it in for this girl. They said the same thing every time. They wanted her fired. Besides the fact that she really didn't do anything wrong, these people didn't realize that we didn't have any other employees. Keeping personnel was always a problem at this store, because nobody who worked in this particular area could afford to live anywhere near it, and the people who lived near the store would not be caught dead working for a living. Even the teenagers we had working there would say, "I'm just working here, because my mom says it will build character." Then they would drive home in their new "beemers". They don't need the money, their parents give them whatever they want.

So, here we were with this snooty couple. The thing that irked me the most is the fact that they would keep going up to her for service at the deli, even if there was someone else working back there. They would always go to her! They just had nothing else to do with themselves than to rant about this girl. Luckily, she wasn't fired, but she was transferred to a different store and exchanged for a different employee. After that, the couple seemed to be bored with themselves, when they had nobody else to pick on. They may have been rich on the outside, but they were sure poor on the inside.

That particular store is a cliché. There are so many people trying to live up to an image that they imagine, or that they saw on t.v. It's quite easy to distinguish the difference between the rich, and the rich by default. One aspect in particular is the slew of bought women. There is a constant array of 100 pound women with a twenty pound diamond and professionally installed forty pound boobs. Their faces are stretched tight and their personality is a wisp. Every now and then, they appear with their husbands, who've got twenty or thirty years on them. It seems contrary, but I actually feel bad for them. I guess you get what you pay for.

So, in the end, what is the meaning of it all? Well, it's ironic, that as I am nearing the end of my writing, an older gentleman comes through my line in the express lane. He was stuck behind a lady, with half a basket, on the phone, and paying with a check. After she left, he looked at me and asked, "Does anyone actually follow the sign anymore?" I honestly told him, "Not really". He then told me the truth of the matter. He said, "Then you should take it down." Unfortunately, he's right. I figure that at some point, just like green stamps, and the $2 bill, the express line will eventually dissipate. They might even get rid of us and replace us with "self checkout". But then, you would have nobody to blame for the long lines but yourself. You would have nobody to yell at, and the angry customers in line would be looking at you!

It is an unfortunate part of the selfish society that we live in today, that people are so puffed up, inflated, and full of hot air, that if you even give them a hint that they are wrong or mistaken, you have to shield yourself from the kabloooeee of their burst bubble, or hear the whine, like when you pull on the opening of a balloon and let the air seep out. People should just be themselves, not trying to keep an inflated image of who they really are. If you have to ask the mirror, who is the fairest of them all, then you are caught in your insecurity.

Then, you must be weary that someone doesn't slip you the shiny apple. You will know how fair you really are, when you can walk right by the mirror. Maybe someday, people will be able to tell me to put down the mirror, look me in the face, and say, "Hello, it is nice to see you."

Essentially, I think it comes down to this: People, in all their variations are wonderful in their own way, and troublemakers in another. Besides minding their manners, it would seem to me that most have lost their ability to assess who they are, and where their place in life and society belongs. More important than striving for more, is the need to belong. So many people want more out of life than they have, or that is possible to have. People are trying so hard to stuff too much into their day, and they eventually find out that they can't do it all. It is like those people, who drive slow in the fast lane. They just don't get it. They don't belong there, and they should move over for those who do. Maybe they belonged there at one time, but not anymore. Many people just cannot keep up with their fast paced life.

I see some trying to carry armloads of stuff up to the express lane to squeeze their way in, justifying to themselves and others, that "Yes, I belong here." When in reality, they have grown, and their life is fuller and slower than it used to be, and now, they belong elsewhere. Maybe it's time to move over into the slow lane. You can see it in the faces of the ones who know and understand their place. They are the ones who let others go in front of them, and whose patience is as long as the day.

I did get to meet a nice lady like that. When I finally shuffled along all the other misfits and got to her order, she was happy and content, telling me that she was not in a hurry. She was going to take her time, and eventually make her way home and enjoy her chocolate "Pinwheels", (Mallow-mars on the east coast). So, my advice is to take your time, enjoy the people around you, and don't spend too much of your life in the fast lane.

As I compile all my thoughts, actions, and experiences, I cannot help but think that I am forgetting something. Every day that goes by, I remember another anecdote, brought on by another event that I add to the list of my adventures. At the same time, new people and experiences are entering my life daily, so I guess in the end, I will someday end up writing a sequel called 15 items or less!

P.S., I forgot to tell you my grocery store jokes. I tend to dish these off on people, who are buying these particular items:

— You had better be careful. You know what happens if you eat too much mayonnaise? You will end up in the Mayo Clinic!

— You had better watch out. You know what happens if you eat too much watermelon? (or any other melon on sale) You will get melon-noma!

— (When purchasing strange foods) You know, in some countries, they eat dog meat! Do you know what they call that? Rin-Din-Din!

This next one I kind of have to set up for those not from my area. There is a little town in the local mountains called

Julian. They are known for their apples, and of course, their apple pies. To get to this cute little town, you have to pass through a larger city at the bottom of the mountain called Ramona. So, at our particular store and others in the area, we carry a selection of pies from a company called Julian Pies. They are wonderful, and by the way, they ship Fed Ex! So, when someone buys one of these pies I say to them:

—You have to be careful with this pie, because you know what happens if you drop a Julian Pie, don't you? (wait for puzzled response) You will end up with Ramona cobbler!

That one always cracks up the locals, but gets a dry grin from people, who don't really know the area, or who have never had cobbler. Sorry, I thought it was funny!

Well, good night everyone, and thank you for shopping with us.

Scott O.

Serving you for 25 years

CLOSING REMARKS

Good morning, it's good to see you again. After 25 years of working at the supermarket, I cannot help but to offer some sort of greeting.

In sunny Southern California, it all began for me when I turned 16 and started searching for my first real job. A family friend, who was the manager at a local supermarket, suggested that I come to work for him at his store. It paid better than minimum wage at the time, so in 1985 I began my career at the grocery store.

I never would have thought that I would remain for so long, but the pay and benefits were good. Noticing how others lives go up and down with the economy, I realized how consistent life was at the supermarket, because people always have to eat.

So, I remained a faithful employee working my way up through many different positions, including management. Although times change, along with the name on the door, the people remain the same.

Throughout the years, I have met so many wonderful individuals, but I have also seen such unusual behavior. I have always had good stories to tell, but finally, I couldn't take it anymore, and I had to put it all in writing.

So, as I am ending my career in the supermarket, and moving on to new adventures, I hope that my observations and sarcastically dry commentary will enthuse, entertain, and enlighten.

For the most part, I really enjoyed my job, working with the many people I've known throughout the years. Some of my fellow employees and customers have come to be good friends. So, as I close the chapter on this portion of my life, I leave you with chocolate wishes, salutations, and a smile.

Good night everyone.

www.ingramcontent.com/pod-product-compliance
Lightning Source LLC
Chambersburg PA
CBHW061728020426

42331CB00006B/1153